THE GOSPEL OF THE REFORMATION

By the same author:

Peter and the Rock

The Church of Rome at the Bar of History

Salvation, the Bible and Roman Catholicism

The Christian: What It Means to Know and Follow Jesus Christ

Must Jesus Be Lord To Be Savior?

Saving Faith: How Does Rome Define It?

Roman Catholic Tradition: Claims and Contradictions

THE GOSPEL OF THE REFORMATION

Salvation From the Guilt and Power of Sin

William Webster

CHRISTIAN RESOURCES INC.

CHRISTIAN RESOURCES INC.
1505 NW 4th Avenue
Battle Ground, WA 98604

ISBN 1–879737–26–4

Cover: An artist's interpretation of a Reformer's stand against ecclesiastical authorities. Artist unknown.

Cover Design: Mike Rotolo

To my wife, Paula, in appreciation for her devotion as a wife and mother, her friendship which is greatly cherished, her commitment to truth and godliness, her invaluable help in the editing of this work and for her partnership as a laborer for the kingdom of God.

CONTENTS

Foreword

I first became familiar with William Webster's work almost a decade ago, through a tremendous little book entitled *Must Jesus Be Lord to Be Savior?* I greatly appreciated that work, which was a very perceptive expose of antinomian tendencies within modern evangelicalism.

Over the years I have eagerly read other books from Bill Webster's pen and have come to view him as a valiant fellow–soldier in the battle for the clarity and simplicity of the true gospel. I have especially appreciated his tireless efforts to defend the doctrine of justification by faith.

Justification by faith has two bitter enemies. Antinomianism is an abuse of justification by faith, taking this doctrine to the extreme of denying any role for good works whatsoever in the life of the person who is saved. That error downplays the role of sanctification in the saving work of God and tends to turn the grace of God into licentiousness (cf. Jude 4).

But at the opposite end of the spectrum lies the sort of doctrine that makes the redeemed one's personal holiness the ground of justification. This in effect nullifies the biblical doctrine of justification by faith *alone*, because it makes something good in the sinner the reason God accepts that person as righteous. It is essentially a denial that Christ's own perfect righteousness, imputed to the believer, is sufficient for full justification (cf. Rom. 4:1–8). This error is at the heart of the Roman Catholic system.

William Webster, a former Roman Catholic himself, has studied Catholic doctrine carefully, meticulously. He has demonstrated rather definitively in other works that the Roman Catholic Church of today is actually at odds with her

9

own history. But even more important, he sees clearly where Roman Catholicism is at odds with the plain truth of Scripture, and that is what this book is all about.

Webster is deeply concerned, as I am, by the modern push for ecumenical union between Roman Catholics and evangelicals. He understands that no such union can occur until the two groups agree on what Scripture teaches about the gospel. And since the chief differences between Roman Catholicism and historic Protestantism have always been major differences about the gospel, ecumenical unity cannot occur unless these crucial truths are downplayed or deemed nonessential. That is too high a price. Thankfully, William Webster sees the gospel as something worth defending, controversy or no.

Nonetheless this book is written in a gracious and irenic tone, utterly devoid of the kind of uncharitable invective and fiery emotion that have soured so many against most discussions of Catholic–Protestant differences. Webster makes his arguments with clarity, with biblical precision, and with an evident love for those with whom he disagrees. That is why this is such a powerful book.

I recommend this book to anyone—Catholic and Protestant alike—who wants to have a clearer understanding of gospel truth. As you read this work, may your spiritual eyes be opened as never before to the bright light of the gospel of God's grace.

John MacArthur Jr.
Pastor, Grace Community Church
Sun Valley, CA.

Introduction

In his opening chapter to the Romans, the apostle Paul states that 'the gospel is the power of God for salvation' (Rom. 1:16). Few statements can equal this one in importance. Paul is underscoring both the priority and importance of the gospel message. It is by the preaching of the gospel that God has ordained that men and women should hear truth and be brought (through the ministry of the Holy Spirit) into the experience of salvation. The critical importance of the gospel message in the salvation of sinners is further stressed by Paul in the following scriptures:

In Him you also, after listening to the message of truth, *the gospel of your salvation, having also believed, you were sealed in Him* with the Holy Spirit of promise (Eph. 1:13).

Now I make known to you, brethren, *the gospel* which I preached to you, which also you received, in which also you stand, *by which also you are saved*, if you hold fast the word which I preached to you, unless you believed in vain. (1 Cor. 15:1-2).

But we should always give thanks to God for you, brethren beloved by the Lord, because *God has chosen you from the beginning for salvation* through sanctification by the Spirit and faith in the truth. *And it was for this He called you through our gospel,* that you may gain the glory of our Lord Jesus Christ (2 Thes. 2:13-14).

The Gentiles are fellow heirs and fellow members of the body, and fellow *partakers of the promise in Christ Jesus through the gospel* (Eph. 3:6).

Whoever will call upon the name of the Lord will be saved.

How then shall they call upon Him in whom they have not believed? And how shall they believe in Him whom they have not heard? And how sshall they hear without a preacher?...So faith comes from hearing, and hearing by the word of Christ (Rom. 10:13-14, 17).

When the biblical gospel is preached it becomes 'the power of God for salvation.' The importance, then, of a correct gospel message can hardly be overstated. As B.B. Warfield put it:

We must not fail to mark the honour which is thus put by the Ascended Jesus on what we have learned to call by way of eminence, the Truth, or, the Gospel message. Everything is made to turn on that. It lies at the root of all. The Apostle's duty is to open men's eyes. Whatever of salvation may come to men comes subsequently to that and as an outgrowth of that root...Men are in darkness, they need light...The appointed means of breaking this darkness is the proclamation of the Gospel by which alone men's eyes can be opened.[1]

We live in a day when the gospel message is being relentlessly assaulted by two great enemies: legalism and antinomianism. These two errors have confused and deceived many, wreaking spiritual havoc throughout both Roman Catholicism and Evangelical Protestantism.

The sixteenth century witnessed one of the greatest revivals in church history: the Reformation. The Protestant Church was born out of a protest against the entrenched legalism of Roman Catholicism. The Reformers fearlessly preached the gospel bearing witness to the biblical message of the sufficiency of the work of Christ, the grace of God and the full and final authority of scripture. They brought the Church back to the essential and liberating message of justification by faith as defined by the word of God. Since the sixteenth century the Reformation gospel has been the standard of orthodoxy for Protestants. Today however, we find a new interest in Roman Catholicism from of all places, conservative Protestantism, and a willingness to embrace uncritically the teachings of the Church of Rome. This is due in part to the fractured nature of evangelicalism and to an antinomian emphasis which is becoming more and more prevalent in evangelical circles. This has sparked an ongoing debate within evangelicalism as to the nature of saving faith and the meaning of salvation. But renewed interest in Roman Catholicism is motivated by more than a reaction against a liberal and antinomian form of evangelicalism. Given the state of today's culture there are those who desire that all conservative forces within professing Christendom unite in a common battle in the culture war for moral values. Unity is the clarion call of this movement but a unity gained at the expense of truth—in particular the great gospel truths which were articulated by the Protestant Reformers. Those evangelicals who promote such an agenda are short sighted. They have forgotten that scripture declares that the God ordained means of changing a culture is through the clear preaching of the gospel of Christ. But it is at this point where there is so much confusion. The recent ECT Accord (promoted by evangelical Charles Colson and Roman Catholic Richard John Neuhaus) has highlighted this wide spread confusion.

There is a desperate need today for a clarification of the biblical gospel. We need to return to a fearless and uncompromising proclamation of the *fulness* of the truth of the gospel as revealed in scripture. This is what characterized the preaching and teaching of the Reformers. Their gospel message was grounded on the ultimate authority of God's word and God blessed their efforts with an outpouring of his Spirit in great power and conversion. The answer for evangelicals who are concerned about the superficiality of evangelicalism and the state of the culture is not union with or tolerance of the legalistic gospel of Rome but a return to the biblical and Reformation gospel. It is this gospel that much of evangelicalism has abandoned.

This book is an attempt to set forth the biblical (Reformation) teaching of the gospel of salvation. It seeks to assess the teachings of Rome and evangelicalism in light of that message and to challenge us to return to the faithful and consistent proclamation of its truth. What is the gospel and what does scripture mean by salvation? What is the essential salvation message of Jesus Christ himself? And what is the content of the gospel that has been consistently taught by those who have followed in the heritage of the Reformation? These are the fundamental questions which will be addressed in the pages that follow. There will be extensive quotations provided from the writings of the Reformers and major Reformed theologians of the centuries following the Reformation. I ask the reader's indulgence in this, but given the widespread confusion that exists on the nature of the gospel of the Reformation, I felt it was essential that there be an accurate documention of its true teaching.

~ 1 ~

The Biblical Meaning of Salvation

But by His doing you are in Christ Jesus, who became to us wisdom from God and righteousness and sanctification and redemption (1 Corinthians 1:30)

To have a correct understanding of the gospel we must have a proper view of the biblical meaning of salvation. What does scripture teach is God's purpose in salvation? Too often our understanding is limited to the truth of justification and deliverance from hell. While these are wonderful truths, they are but part of the overall work of salvation. When Paul states that the gospel is 'the power of God for salvation' (Rom. 1:16), he is referring not only to deliverance from the guilt of sin and its eternal consequences, but also from its *power* and *dominion* (Rom. 3–8). Paul further emphasizes this in his first letter to the Corinthians where he says: 'But by His doing you are in Christ Jesus, who became to us wisdom from God, and righteousness and sanctification and redemption...And such were some of you; but you were washed, but you were sanctified, but you were justified in the name of our Lord Jesus Christ, and in the Spirit of our God' (1 Cor. 1:30; 6:11). These scriptures make it clear that when these believers came into the experience of salvation they were not only justified but sanctified. In short, the concept of salvation in scripture encompasses divine sovereignty, regeneration, justification, sanctification, adoption, conversion and glorification. It encompasses *all* that God does to deliver a man from the guilt, power and consequences of sin

15

and to restore him into a relationship with himself that he might know, love, worship, obey, serve, and glorify God in time and eternity.

As we will see, this was the view held by the Reformers and all who have followed in the tradition of the Reformation. It is important that we keep this point continually before us: *Salvation means much more than deliverance from condemnation. It means deliverance from sin, not only its guilt but also its dominion and power.* Martyn Lloyd–Jones states:

> The prime object of God in instituting salvation for us in Christ Jesus is not simply that we might be forgiven. This is how Paul puts it in his letter to the Ephesians, 'We are His workmanship, created in Christ Jesus'. What for? '...unto good works, which God hath before ordained that we should walk in them' (2:10). Or again, in his Epistle to Titus: 'Who gave himself for us'. Why did He do it? '...that He might redeem us from all iniquity, and purify unto himself a peculiar people zealous for good works' (2:14). You cannot stop at forgiveness. Christ died to do all this; and all this must be stated in our evangelism. It must also become apparent at once in the life of the believer. Indeed everything about the Gospel inevitably leads to this end.[2]

A.A. Hodge makes this observation:

> The very end for which the stupendous enginery of redemption was devised and executed, including the incarnation, crucifixion, resurrection of the Son of God, and the mission of the Holy Ghost, is to establish a community of regenerated and sanctified men, absolutely perfect in righteousness.[3]

John Murray likewise emphasizes the importance of understanding the overall intent of Christ in his work of redemption:

⟨The ultimate goal of the whole redemptive process both in its objective accomplishment and in its application is conformity to the image of Christ.⟩All the steps are subordinated to this purpose—they flow out of it and move to its realization. Christ gave himself a ransom that he might deliver his people from all iniquity. Justification is only one part or aspect of this redemptive process and must never be viewed in disjunction from its place in the context of all the other steps of the process and particularly the other aspects of the application of redemption. Any doctrine out of focus gives distortion to the whole system of truth and is therefore inimical to the ethical interests to be promoted by that system of truth. Redemption is unto holiness and justification as a part of that process of redemption cannot be to the opposite end.[4]

Christ came as the God–Man, the Mediator between God and man, to deliver us from sin—from its guilt, power and condemnation. He came to deliver us from the power and authority of Satan and eternal death and to bring us to God (1 Pet. 3:18, Jn. 17:3).

If salvation means deliverance from sin, then it is obvious that a proper understanding of it entails a thorough understanding of the nature of sin and the subsequent means God employs in delivering man from it.

~ 2 ~

Man's Need for Salvation

For all have sinned and fall short of the glory of God (Romans 3:23)

Scripture teaches that we were created *by* God, *for* God (Col. 1:16). We were created for a purpose—his glory. The law of God is God's revelation of his purpose in creating man. It teaches us thatGod is meant to have first place in our hearts and his will is meant to be the controlling principle of our lives. The law of God reveals two categories of relationship for which men are accountable: 1) *To God as a person*: we are commanded to love him with all our hearts and to have no other gods before him (Ex. 20:2–3; Mt. 22:37) and 2) *To God's will:* we are commanded to obey him in our thoughts, words, motives, attitudes and actions. Man's relationship with God is meant to be characterized by submission of heart, dependence, love, devotion, worship, obedience and service—all directed to his glory. As John Murray states: 'It is the law that expresses the nature and will of the supreme personality who has authority over us and propriety in us, to whom we owe complete submission and absolute devotion.'[5] We have been created to love him supremely and to live a life of submission to him and obedience to his will for his glory. This purpose is not only revealed in the law of God but also in the person of Christ.

The Lord Jesus Christ was a perfect man. In his life we find the perfect prototype of what man was created to be. In Jesus we find what it means to have a true heart towards God.

Philippians 2:6–7 helps us to understand the human nature of Jesus. It says: 'Who, although He existed in the form of God, did not regard equality with God a thing to be grasped, but emptied Himself, taking the form of a bondservant, and being made in the likeness of men.' The word *form* means the innate nature or character of a thing. The word *bondservant* is the Greek word *doulos*. At the incarnation, in taking upon himself the nature of man, Jesus took upon himself the *form* of a bondservant. This is the innate character of his nature as a man. God predestines those he chooses 'to become conformed to the image of His Son' (Rom. 8:29) and his Son became a bondslave. This truth has direct bearing on the preaching of the gospel and our understanding of salvation for salvation ultimately means being conformed to the image of Christ. As we investigate in more detail the application and appropriation of salvation we will be referring back to this truth.

The Law of God and the Nature of Sin

The law of God is the expression of his will for man. All men are 'under the law' in their natural state (Rom. 3:19) and accountable to the law as responsible moral agents. And what the law of God requires of us is perfect obedience in all our behavior—in our attitudes, thoughts, motives, speech and actions. If we transgress God's law in any respect we are condemned, placed under the judgment and wrath of God and face the destiny of an eternal hell when we die: 'Cursed is everyone who does not abide by all things written in the book of the law to perform them...The wages of sin is death...The soul who sins will die' (Gal. 3:10; Rom. 6:23; Ezek. 18:4). Scripture sums up our true condition before God when it says: All have sinned and fall short of the glory of God' (Rom. 3:23).

Scripture teaches that we are all sinners, born in a state of sin—of rebellion against God—in which we live unto ourselves as our own authority, independent of God (Is. 53:6).

We are born separated from God and at enmity with him in our nature (Eph. 2:12; Col. 1:21; Rom. 8:7–8). We are idolators. We worship, love and serve other gods in God's place. Self–love, self–will, and self–rule are the governing principles of our hearts. God has been displaced by self. Our sinful nature then manifests itself in behavioral sins which are contrary to the law and word of God. We are not rightly related to God in our nature or behavior. We are therefore creatures whose lives are not only characterized by sin, but are in bondage to its guilt and power. Scripture describes us as unrighteous, ungodly, enemies of God, slaves of sin, evil in heart and life and the children of Satan (Jn. 8:34; Rom. 6:19; Lk. 11:13; 1 Jn. 3:4–10). As Isaiah 53:6 puts it: 'All of us like sheep have gone astray, each of us has turned to his own way.' Or as Romans 3:10–12 states: 'There is none righteous no not one, there is none who understands, there is none who seeks for God, all have turned aside, together they have become useless, there is none who does good, there is not even one.' And because we are sinners we have incurred guilt before God and are under the curse of the law which is eternal death.

Scripture is emphatic—all men are sinners. However, it is important to emphasize a crucial point with respect to sin: *The first and foremost issue in defining sin is not with particular acts of behavior but with the disposition of the heart in relation to the person of God himself.* If we define sin in terms of behavior only we will miss the fundamental purpose behind the salvation Christ came to accomplish. Sin first of all has to do with the heart and only secondarily with acts of behavior. Sin in its essence is not being submitted to God, not loving him supremely, not living exclusively for his glory, not having him as the center of one's life. It is to love self, to live for self and to have self at the center of the life. J.I. Packer defines sin in these terms:

> What in positive terms is the essence of sin? Playing God; and as a means to this, refusing to allow the Creator to be God so far as you are concerned. Living, not for Him, but for

yourself; loving and serving and pleasing yourself without reference to the Creator, trying to be as far as possible independent of Him, taking yourself out of His hands, holding Him at arm's length, keeping the reins of life in your own hands; acting as if you, and your pleasure, were the end to which all things else, God included, must be made to function as a means. That is the attitude in which sin essentially consists...Sin is exalting oneself against the Creator, withholding the homage due to Him, and putting oneself in His place, as the ultimate standard of reference in all life's decisions...Where Christ does not rule sin does.[6]

Again, we cannot understand the true nature of salvation apart from a correct understanding of sin. As J.C. Ryle has stated: 'A right knowledge of sin lies at the root of all saving Christianity.'[7] Jonathan Edwards comments on the primary meaning of sin as a state of being which then produces sinful acts:

The apostasy of man summarily consists in departing from the true God, to idols; forsaking his Creator, and setting up other things in his room. When God at first created man, he was united to his Creator; the God that made him was his God. The true God was the object of his highest respect, and had the possession of his heart. Love to God was the principle in his heart, that ruled over all other principles; and everything in the soul was wholly in subjection to it. But when man fell, he departed from the true God, and the union that was between his heart and his Creator was broken: he wholly lost his principle of love to God. And henceforth man clave to other gods. He gave that respect to the creature, which is due to the Creator. When God ceased to be the object of his supreme love and respect, other things of course became the objects of it.

The gods which a natural man worships, instead of the God that made him, are himself and the world. He has withdrawn his esteem and honour from God, and proudly exalts himself.

As Satan was not willing to be in subjection; and therefore rebelled, and set up himself; so a natural man, in the proud and high thoughts he has of himself, sets up himself upon God's throne. He gives his heart to the world, worldly riches, worldly pleasures, and worldly honours: they have the possession of that regard which is due to God.[8]

According to the world we are all brothers and sisters, children of God. But scripture teaches that men in their unregenerate state are actually children of Satan, citizens of the kingdom of this world and as such are under Satan's power and authority (Jn. 8:41–44; Eph. 2:1–2). The heart of Satan is pride, self–rule self–will. It is *this* fundamental disposition which is the root and essence of sin. Man is in bondage to the guilt and power of sin and is therefore subject to death—physical, spiritual and eternal (Gal. 3:10; Ezek. 18:4; Rom. 6:23). Man is under a curse, the ultimate judgment of which is eternal separation from God in hell.

~ 3 ~

Judgment and Hell

And I saw a great white throne and Him who sat upon it, from whose presence earth and heaven fled away, and no place was found for them. And I saw the dead, the great and the small, standing before the throne, and the books were opened, and another book was opened, which is the book of life; and the dead were judged from the things which were written in the books, according to their deeds...And if anyone's name was not found written in the book of life, he was thrown into the lake of fire (Revelation 20:11–12, 15)

The word of God warns there is a day of judgment coming when all men will stand before God. Hebrews 9:27 states: 'And inasmuch as it is appointed for men to die once and after this comes judgment.' The judgment of God is an inescapable reality, so any discussion of judgment must include an examination of the subject of hell.

Our Creator is a God of love and mercy. But he is also a God of wrath and a righteous judge because he is a God of infinite holiness. Over and over again scripture emphasizes these truths about our Creator:

God is light and in Him there is no darkness at all (1 Jn. 1:5).

Holy, holy, holy is the Lord God, the Almighty, who was and who is and who is to come (Rev. 4:8).

Let the heavens be glad and the earth rejoice...before the Lord for He is coming; for He is coming to judge the earth. He will judge the world in righteousness, and the peoples in

25

His faithfulness (Ps. 96:11–13).

The wrath of God is revealed from heaven against all ungodliness and unrighteousness of men (Rom. 1:18).

God is now declaring to men that all everywhere must repent for He has fixed a day in which He will judge the world in righteousness (Acts 17:30–31).

God will bring to account every thought, word and deed. He is omniscient—he knows us through and through:

There is no creature hidden from his sight, but all things are open and laid bare to the eyes of him with whom we have to do (Heb. 4:13).

His eyes are upon the ways of man. He sees all his steps (Job 34:21).

Every man's way is clean in his own eyes but the Lord weighs the motives (Prov. 16:3).

You are those who justify yourselves in the sight of men but God knows your hearts...(Lk. 16:15).

Every careless word that men shall speak they shall render account of it in the day of judgment (Mt. 12:36).

God knows our hearts. What goes on *within* us matters to God. Jesus made this clear when he said: 'I say to you, that everyone who looks on a woman to lust for her has committed adultery with her already in his heart' (Mt. 5:28). As far as God is concerned—to think it is to do it. He *hates* sin and his anger is expressed in what scripture calls the wrath of God—a wrath that is revealed in the course of this life, and which will be fully revealed at the day of judgment:

The wrath of God is revealed from heaven against all ungodliness and unrighteousness of men (Rom. 1:18).

Do you think lightly of the riches of His kindness and forbearance and patience not knowing that the kindness of God leads you to repentance. But because of your stubborness and unrepentant heart you are storing up wrath for yourself in the day of wrath and revelation of the righteous judgment of God, who will render to every man according to his deeds (Rom. 2:4-6).

When the Lord Jesus shall be revealed from heaven with His mighty angels in flaming fire, dealing out retribution to those who do not know God and to those who do not obey the gospel of our Lord Jesus. And these will pay the penalty of eternal destruction away from the presence of the Lord and from the glory of His power when He comes to be glorified in His saints on that day (2 Thes. 1:7-9).

And they said to the mountains and rocks, fall on us and hide us from the presence of Him who sits on the throne and from the wrath of the Lamb, for the great day of their wrath has come and who is able to stand (Rev. 6:16).

Because God is holy and just he *must* judge and punish sin. If we want to know God's evaluation of sin we need look no further than the cross of Christ. The cross is a public display of God's judgment against sin. God is a God of wrath and judgment and there is coming a great and terrible day of the Lord for all of those outside of Jesus Christ:

The sun will be turned into darkness and the moon to blood before the great and awesome day of the Lord comes (Joel 2:31).

And angels who did not keep their domain, but abandoned their proper abode, He has kept in eternal bonds under darkness for the judgment of the great day (Jude 6).

The Teaching of Jesus

Hell is a reality; a real and physical place—eternal in duration. In hell, both soul and body will be confined, separated from God in unspeakable and unimaginable torment.

There are three major words in the New Testament which are used to describe hell: Hades, the Lake of Fire and Gehenna. The word Gehenna is the most thoroughly descriptive of what hell is like. John Blanchard gives us some historical background to this word:

> About 750 B.C. King Ahaz was ruler of Judah. A spineless idolater, he adopted some of the most revolting heathen practices of his day. Among the worst was the offering of human sacrifices—he even had his own sons burned to death. These atrocities were carried out in the valley of Ben Hinnom, a place just south–west of Jerusalem and today called Wadi al–Rababi. Ahaz paid dearly for his sin. His political alliances came unstuck and in one battle he lost 120,000 men. His place was taken by the godly King Hezekiah, but he was succeeded in turn by his son Manasseh, who undid all the good his father had done. He rebuilt altars to heathen idols, reinstituted human sacrifices and, like Ahaz, burned his own sons to death, again in the valley of Ben Hinnom. Manasseh was followed by his equally corrupt son Amon, who lasted only two years before being assassinated.
>
> His eight year old son Josiah took his place, and by the time he was sixteen he had begun a programme of vigorous reformation. Altars were torn down, images were smashed, and the pieces scattered over the graves of those who had bowed down to them in worship. In his crusade Josiah singled out the valley of Ben Hinnom for particular attention. From being a place of idol worship he turned it into a public rubbish dump in which all the offal and filth of Jerusalem was poured. Later, the bodies of animals and even the corpses of criminals were flung there and left to rot or to be consumed by the fire that was kept constantly burning to dispose of the stinking mass of garbage. As one writer comments, it was a place where 'the fires never stopped burning and the worms never stopped eating.' We can now see how this otherwise unimportant piece of land fits into the picture. The Hebrew place–name was originally Ge(ben)hinnom (the valley of the sons of Hinnom). The shortened form of the name was Ge–hinnom of which the Greek translation became Gehenna. The English word for Gehenna, with all its imagery of shame,

disgrace, sin, guilt, judgment and punishment, is 'hell.'[9]

Fire is the word used most often in scripture to describe hell. Gehenna is the place where the fire never ceases to burn. The word Gehenna is used twelve times in the New Testament with eleven of those by Jesus himself. John the Baptist gives this description of Jesus Christ as Judge: 'His winnowing fork is in His hand, and He will thoroughly clear His threshing floor, and He will gather His wheat into the barn, but He will burn up the chaff with unquenchable fire' (Mt. 3:12). The book of Revelation predicts that at the last judgment 'if anyone's name was not found written in the book of life, he was thrown into the lake of fire' (Rev. 20:15). The image of an eternal unceasing fire graphically depicts the agony and torment of hell. The descriptions of hell recorded in scripture are terrifying. They are *meant* to terrify us. The Lord Jesus had a great deal to say about hell which is calculated to sober and warn us:

But I say to you that everyone who is angry with his brother shall be guilty before the court; and whoever shall say to his brother, 'Raca,' shall be guilty before the supreme court, and whoever shall say 'You fool,' shall be guilty enough to go into the fiery hell (Mt. 5:22).

And if your right eye makes you stumble, tear it out, and throw it from you; for it is better for you that one of the parts of your body perish, than for your whole body to be thrown into hell (Mt. 5:29).

And if your hand causes you to stumble, cut it off; it is better for you to enter life crippled, than having your two hands, to go into hell, into the unquenchable fire, where their worm does not die, and their fire is not quenched (Mk. 9:43-44).

But when the Son of Man comes in His glory, and all the angels with Him, then He will sit on His glorious throne...Then He will say to those on His left, 'Depart from Me, accursed ones, into the eternal fire which has been prepared for the devil and his angels...And these will go away into eternal punishment, but the righteous into eternal life (Mt. 25:31,41,46).

Therefore just as the tares are gathered up and burned with fire, so shall it be at the end of the age. The Son of Man will send forth His angels, and they will gather out of His kingdom all stumbling blocks, and those who commit lawlessness, and will cast them into the furnace of fire; in that place there shall be weeping and gnashing of teeth (Mt. 13:40–42; Cf. Mt. 13:49–50).

Do not fear those who kill the body, but are unable to kill the soul; but rather fear Him who is able to destroy both soul and body in hell (Mt. 10:28).

You serpents, you brood of vipers, how shall you escape the sentence of hell (Mt. 23:33)?

No one who takes these teachings of Jesus seriously can fail to be greatly sobered by his words. Hell is a place of unending torment—a place of weeping and gnashing of teeth, of darkness, isolation, despair—of unceasing suffering and pain. John Calvin provides this commentary on hell:

Now, because no description can deal adequately with the gravity of God's vengeance against the wicked, their torments and tortures are figuratively expressed to us by physical things, that is, by darkness, weeping, and gnashing of teeth (Matt. 8:12; 22:13), unquenchable fire (Matt. 3:12; Mark 9:43; Isa. 66:24), an undying worm gnawing at the heart (Isa. 66:24). By such expressions the Holy Spirit certainly intended to confound all our senses with dread: as when he speaks of 'a deep Gehenna prepared from eternity, fed with fire and much wood; the breath of the Lord, like a stream of brimstone, kindles it' (Isa. 30:33). As by such details we should be enabled in some degree to conceive the lot of the wicked, so we ought especially to fix our thoughts upon this: how wretched it is to be cut off from all fellowship with God. And not that only but to feel his sovereign power against you that you cannot escape being pressed by it. For first, his displeasure is like a raging fire, devouring and engulfing everything it touches. Secondly, all creatures so serve him in the execution of his judgment that they to whom the Lord will openly show his wrath will feel heaven, earth, sea, living beings, and all that exists aflame, as it were, with dire anger against them, and armed to destroy them. Accordingly, it was no insignificant thing that the apostle declared when he said that the faithless 'shall suffer the punishment of eternal destruction, excluded from the presence of the Lord and from the glory of his might' (II Thes. 1:9)...Consequently, unhappy consciences find no rest from being troubled and tossed by a terrible whirlwind, from feeling that they are being torn asunder by a hostile Deity, pierced and lanced by deadly darts, quaking at God's lightning bolt, and being crushed by the weight of his hand—so that it would be more bearable to go down into any bottomless depths and chasms than to stand for a moment in these terrors.[10]

Each of us will die one day and we will enter eternity where we will live forever. Scripture declares that we will be in one of two places: in heaven or hell. There is no teaching in scripture about purgatory. Once we die it is too late to rectify our situation if we have not faced and dealt with our sinful state before God. We are warned to be prepared to meet our God. Thankfully, he has provided a way for us to be prepared to meet him and to be rescued from eternal judgment through his Son. This is in part why the gospel is called good news. Through Jesus Christ, we can stand before God with confidence rather than dread. In Christ, we can be delivered from the guilt and power of sin and from this eternal hell. We can receive forgiveness and eternal life. This is the good news of the gospel. But in sharing the gospel which makes these promises we must also preach fearlessly against sin, warning men that they must turn from sin to Christ and flee the wrath of God that is to come (Mt. 3:7–8). Those who reject the gospel of Christ and die in sin will suffer eternally in hell.

~ 4 ~

The Source of Salvation

I am the bread of life; he who comes to Me shall not hunger,
and he who believes in Me shall never thirst (John 6:35)

We are all sinners separated from God. Because of this we are faced with a hopeless situation apart from the intervention of God. Thankfully, he has intervened. In mercy and love he has provided a Savior to deliver us from sin and its consequences and to restore us to a relationship with himself that he might fulfil in us the purpose for which we were created. The person and work of Jesus Christ is God's answer to the problem of man's sin. It is through Christ *alone* that we find deliverance. Jesus emphasized this when he stated: 'I am the way, and the truth, and the life; no one comes to the Father, but through Me' (Jn. 14:6). The apostle Peter reiterated it with these words: 'And there is salvation in no one else; for there is no other name under heaven that has been given among men, by which we must be saved' (Acts 4:12). But while it is necessary to know and embrace the historical and biblical facts about the person and work of Jesus Christ, the facts alone are not enough to save. We have been called to a personal relationship with the *person* of Christ. It is this aspect of salvation that I want to focus on here. God's means of saving lost men and women is through a *personal relationship* with his Son. The biblical description of this relationship is *union with Christ*. Understanding this is foundational to a biblical understanding of salvation and it is key to understanding the gospel preached by the Reformers.

Union With Christ

All the benefits of our salvation are communicated to us through union with Christ. Outside of this union there is no salvation. Paul's favorite phrase to describe salvation is 'in Christ.' Salvation is a person, the Lord Jesus Christ. And an individual is saved when he comes into a right relation with Christ as a person. If a man is 'in Christ' he will experience salvation: justification, sanctification, adoption, regeneration, reconciliation, redemption, forgiveness, conversion and glorification. Scripture emphasizes the necessity of this union with Christ in order to partake of the benefits of salvation in the following verses:

> But by His doing you are in Christ Jesus who became to us wisdom from God and righteousness and sanctification and redemption (1 Cor. 1:30).
>
> But God being rich in mercy, because of His great love with which He loved us, even when we were dead in our transgressions, made us alive together with Christ (Eph. 2:4-5).
>
> In Him we have redemption through His blood, the forgiveness of our trespasses (Eph. 1:7).
>
> Therefore my brethren you also were made to die to the Law through the body of Christ that you might be joined to another to Him who was raised from the dead that you might bear fruit for God (Rom. 7:4).

The Reformers and Reformed theologians who have followed them all speak with one accord regarding the necessity for union with Christ for salvation:

John Calvin: Christ was given to us by God's generosity, to be grasped and possessed by us in faith. By partaking of him, we principally receive a double grace: namely, that being reconciled to God through Christ's blamelessness, we may have in heaven instead of a Judge a gracious Father; and secondly, that sanctified by Christ's spirit we may cultivate blamelessness and purity of life.[11]...That thus engrafted into him (cf. Rom. 11:19) we are already, in a manner, partakers of eternal life, having entered in the Kingdom of God through hope[12]...I confess that we are deprived of this utterly incomparable good until Christ is made ours. Therefore, that joining together of Head and members, that indwelling of Christ in our hearts—in short, that mystical union—are accorded by us the highest degree of importance, so that Christ, having been made ours, makes us sharers with him in the gifts with which he has been endowed. We do not, therefore, contemplate him outside ourselves from afar in order that his righteousness may be imputed to us but because we put on Christ and are grafted into his body—in short, because he deigns to make us one with him. For this reason, we glory that we have fellowship of righteousness with him.[13]

Heinrich Bullinger (Swiss Reformer): First of all the evangelical and apostolic doctrine teaches us that Christ is joined to us by his Spirit, and that we are tied to him in mind or spirit by faith, that he may live in us and we in him. For the Lord cries out in the Gospel saying: 'If any man thirst, let him come to me and drink. He that believeth in me (as the scripture saith) shall have streams of living water flowing out of his body...Christ our Lord is joined unto us in spirit, and we are tied to him in mind and faith, as the body to the head. Therefore those who lack this knot and bond, that is, who have not the Spirit of Christ, nor true faith in Christ, are not true and lively members of Christ...[14]

Martin Luther: The third incomparable benefit of faith is that it unites the soul with Christ as a bride is united with her bridegroom. By this mystery, as the Apostle teaches, Christ and the soul become one flesh (Eph. 5:31-32). And if they are one flesh and there is between them a true marriage...it follows that everything they have they hold in common, the good as well as the evil. Accordingly the believing soul can boast of and glory in whatever Christ has as though it were its own...[15]

John Owen: Whatever is wrought in believers by the Spirit of Christ, it is their *union* to the person of Christ, and by virtue thereof...By him we are united unto Christ–that is, his person, and not a light within us, as some think; nor the doctrine of the gospel, as others with an equal folly seem to imagine. It is by the doctrine and grace of the gospel that we are united, but it is the person of Christ whereunto we are united.[16]

Louis Berkhof: Since the believer is 'a new creature' (2 Cor. 5:17), or 'is justified' (Acts 13:39) only in Christ, union with Him logically precedes both regeneration and justification by faith, while yet, chronologically, the moment when we are united with Christ is also the moment of our regeneration and justification.[17]

R.L. Dabney: It is through this union to Christ that the whole application of redemption is effectuated on the sinner's soul. Although all the fulness of the Godhead dwelleth bodily in Him since His glorification, yet until the union with Christ is effected, the believer partakes of none of its completeness. When made one with His Redeeming Head, then all the communicable graces of that Head begin to transfer themselves to him. Thus we find that each kind of benefit which makes up redemption is, in different parts of Scripture, deduced from this union as their source; justification, spiritual strength, life, resurrection of the body, good works, prayer and praise, sanctification, perseverance, &c.[18]

Scripture is unequivocal: the person of Christ alone is the source of salvation and union with him is God's means of applying that salvation to men. Many wrongly believe that the application of salvation is a result of faith, but this is not what scripture teaches. The word of God teaches that faith unites one to Christ and as a result of that union the individual experiences salvation. The all important truth that scripture teaches is that salvation comes from a *relationship* with Christ. This means that salvation is not only justification. When an individual is justified he is automatically and invariably sanctified because both benefits flow from union with Christ. We cannot, therefore, separate justification from sanctification. But such an affirmation does not mean that we are *equating* sanctification with justification. The two are completely different concepts which need to be carefully distinguished. Sanctification is *not* the basis upon which an individual is justified. Nonetheless it is a scriptural truth that God justifies no one whom he does not at the same time sanctify. It is important that we clearly understand a number of principles as they relate to union with Christ and salvation. First of all, we must understand that God is able to justify an individual from sin through union with Christ because Christ has accomplished a work of salvation. So we must thoroughly understand that work. Secondly, we must understand the biblical requirements for entering into a saving relationship with Christ. We will begin by looking in detail at justification and the work of Christ, and then at repentance and faith.

~ 5 ~

Justification

Being justified as a gift by His grace through the redemption which is in Christ Jesus; whom God displayed publicly as a propitiation in His blood through faith...A man is justified by faith apart from the works of the Law (Romans 3:24–25, 28)

One of the great truths of salvation is that of justification. But what is justification? The heart of the Reformation controversy was over the meaning of this word and despite the impression given by ECT, the Roman Catholic and Protestant Churches are still very much at odds with one another on this issue.

The Reformers claimed that the Roman Catholic Church had perverted the true biblical meaning of the term by insisting on the necessity of works and sacraments as the basis for justification. And the Roman Church charged that the Reformer's teaching of faith alone (*sola fide*) and imputed righteousness was unbiblical and itself a perversion of the gospel message. For a proper evaluation of these two positions it is essential that we understand correctly what the *bible* teaches on this subject. And this begins with a biblical understanding of the nature of God. Why? Because all biblical teaching on salvation is rooted in the character of God himself.

The Nature of God

Scripture declares that God is a God of holiness. He is a God of light in whom there is no darkness at all (1 Jn. 1:5). Because he is holy, he is just. He always acts righteously and in accord with his law since the law is an expression of his essential character. His holiness demands just dealings with sin. Thus, scripture teaches that the one true and living God is a God of wrath and judgment precisely because he is a God of holiness. As Leon Morris puts it:

> The Old Testament consistently thinks of a God who works by the method of Law. This is not the conception of one or two writers but is found everywhere in the Old Testament...Yahweh was thought of as essentially righteous in His nature, as incorporating the law of righteousness within His essential Being. Accordingly He works by a method which may be called law—He inevitably punishes evil–doing and rewards righteousness. He Himself acts righteously, and He demands that His people do the same.[19]

This is confirmed in the New Testament by the apostle Paul where he states that the atonement of Christ takes place to vindicate the righteousness of God, so that he might be found *just* while mercifully justifying sinners:

> Being justified as a gift by His grace through the redemption which is in Christ Jesus; whom God displayed publicly as a propitiation in His blood through faith. This was to demonstrate His righteousness, because in the forbearance of God He passed over sins previously committed; for the demonstration, I say, of His righteousness at the present time, that He might be just and the justifier of the one who has faith in Jesus (Rom. 3:24-26).

This passage tells us something very significant about God and forgiveness. It tells us that God is a God of love and mercy but that he cannot and will not exercise his mercy in a way that would compromise his justice and righteousness. He *must* act in accord with his law because it is an expression of his holiness. So the forgiveness and justification of sinners must be compatible with God's justice and righteousness. It must be consistent with and in fulfillment of his law. And that means that he must judge sin. So the ultimate question is this: How can unjust sinners stand before the judgment of a God who is infinitely holy and just? God, in his love, desires to forgive us and to extend mercy, but he cannot do so if it compromises his holiness and justice.

The law demands death for transgression and perfect obedience for God's acceptance. How can he forgive and accept us when we have transgressed the law and consequently do not possess this perfect righteousness?

This is why the gospel is good news. It tells us that God has provided a salvation for us in his Son, the Lord Jesus Christ. He has provided a means of redeeming us that is consistent with his holy nature and law. He is able to exercise his love and extend to us forgiveness without compromising his holiness and justice.

The great message of the gospel is that we can be justified (forgiven and accepted by God) by grace through faith on account of Christ. The Protestant and Roman Catholic Churches both agree with this statement but define the terms differently. The key to understanding this difference in interpretation is the word *alone*. The Protestant Church states that an individual is justified by grace *alone*, through faith *alone*, on account of Christ *alone*. This distinction is crucial in understanding the scriptural teaching of justification because the word *alone* safeguards its biblical meaning. To omit this important word is to distort the scriptural teaching on justification.

There are four key concepts expressed by this summary statement of the gospel: Justification, grace, faith and on account of Christ. To understand the first three—justification, grace and faith—we must understand that last phrase—on account of Christ, because scripture makes a direct correlation between justification and the work of Christ. If we understand the work of Christ we will understand the meaning of faith, grace and justification. Any meaningful discussion of justification must be based upon a thorough understanding of the atonement of Christ.

The Work of Christ in Atonement

One of the most important elements in understanding the atonement is its relationship to the law. The word of God states that Christ undertook the work of atonement to deal with the penalty of a transgressed law. In so doing he becomes both a *curse* and a *propitiation*. Thus, the atonement is forensic in nature because it is judicial in nature. This is emphasized in Paul's letters to the Galatians and Romans:

> For as many as are the works of the law are under a *curse*; for it is written, 'Cursed is everyone who does not abide by all things written in the book of the Law to perform them.' Now that no one is justified by the Law before God is evident; for, 'The righteous man shall live by faith.' However, the Law is not of faith; on the contrary, 'He who practices them shall live by them.' Christ redeemed us from the *curse* of the Law, having become a *curse* for us—for it is written, 'Cursed is everyone who hangs on a tree' (Gal. 3:10–13).
>
> But now apart from the Law the righteousness of God has been manifested, being witnessed by the Law and the prophets, even the righteousness of God through faith in Jesus Christ for all those who believe; for there is no distinction; for all have sinned and fall short of the glory of God, being justified as a gift by His grace through the redemption which is in Christ Jesus; whom God displayed publicly as a propitiation in His blood through faith. This was to demonstrate His righteousness, because in the forbearance of God He passed over the sins previously committed. For the demonstration I say of His righteousness at the present time that He might be just and the justifier of the one who has faith in Jesus. Where then is boasting? It is excluded. By what kind of law? Of works? No, but by a law of faith. For

we maintain that a man is justified by faith apart from the works of the Law (Rom. 3:21–28).

There are four important concepts emphasized in these passages which are key to an understanding of the New Testament doctrine of the atonement of Christ: The phrase 'For us'; Curse; Propitiation; The righteousness of God

For Us

The scriptures tell us that Christ became a curse *for us*. This is the truth of substitution. Jesus became a curse by bearing man's sin and taking man's place as his substitute to suffer the punishment due those sins by enduring the penalty of God's broken law in man's place. All of our sin was imputed to him and the judgment of God in all its fury came upon him:

> God demonstrates His own love towards us, in that while we were yet sinners, *Christ died for us* (Rom. 5:8).
> Grace to you and peace from God our Father and the Lord Jesus Christ, *who gave Himself for our sins*, that He might deliver us out of this present evil age (Gal. 1:3–4).
> He Himself *bore our sins* in His body on the cross (1 Pet. 2:24).
> He was pierced through *for our transgressions*, He was crushed *for our iniquity*. The chastening for our well being fell upon Him and by His scourging we are healed. All of us like sheep have gone astray, each of us has turned to his own way, but the Lord has caused the iniquity of us all to fall on Him (Is. 53:4-6).
> He made Him who knew no sin *to be sin on our behalf* (2 Cor. 5:21).

Curse and Propitiation

Our sin was imputed to Christ. He then became a propitiation, suffering the wrath of God against our sin by laying down his own life in death to satisfy the demands of the law. This is the primary meaning of the word propitiation—to satisfy wrath. In this case it refers specifically to the wrath of God in relation to sin. Christ bore the wrath of God as a judgment against sin. This underscores the fact that Christ's atonement is penal in nature. It relates to the law of God. Scripture teaches that one of the purposes of Christ's incarnation was related to the law of God: 'But when the fulness of time came, God sent forth His Son, born of a woman, born under the Law, in order that He might redeem those who were under the Law, that we might receive the adoption as sons' (Gal. 4:4–5). On the cross Christ bore the full punishment of the law as man's substitute. In becoming a propitiation, he completely satisfied the justice of God in that full punishment has been meted out to Christ as our substitute. He bore the full penalty of the law—the curse of the law (he hangs on a tree in death)—because the law demands death for transgression. The reference to the shedding of blood in scripture as the payment for sin always represents a life laid down in death. There are various descriptions of this in the New Testament: 'Christ...gave Himself for our sins (Gal. 1:4); He...delivered Him up for us all (Rom. 8:32); Christ also loved you and gave Himself up for us, an offering and a sacrifice to God (Eph. 5:2); But God demonstrated His own love towards us, in that while we were yet sinners Christ died for us (Rom. 5:8); In Him we have redemption through His blood, the forgiveness of our trespasses (Eph. 1:7).' These expressions refer us back to the Old Testament sacrificial system which represented the ultimate sacrifice of Christ as the lamb of God:

For the life of the flesh is in the blood and I have given it to you on the altar to make an atonement for your souls, for it is the blood by reason of the life that makes atonement (Lev. 17:11).

Without the shedding of blood there is no forgiveness (Heb. 9:27).

Behold the lamb of God who takes away the sin of the world (Jn. 1:29).

So when scripture tells us that we are justified as a gift through the propitiation of Christ and his blood (Rom. 3:25–26; 5:9), it means that through his death he bore our sin and perfectly fulfilled all the requirements of the law as our substitute. If we understand Christ's atonement we will begin to understand the biblical meaning of justification. Justification is directly related to the atonement in scripture: 'Having now been *justified by His blood* we shall be saved from the wrath of God through Him' (Rom. 5:9). To be justified by Christ's blood is to be justified by his death which is his work of atonement.

What then is the nature of Christ's atonement according to the word of God? Christ has borne the *totality* of man's sin. In his one act of obedience as a propitiatory sacrifice in death he has borne the full judgment and condemnation of God against sin forever. The New Testament teaches that his atonement is *once–for–all.* This means that the work of atonement is a finished and complete work. Jesus himself said, 'It is finished.' Note the following references to the *once–for–all* nature of the atonement:

Knowing that Christ, having been raised from the dead, is never to die again; death no longer is master over Him. For the death that He died, He died to sin, *once for all*; but the life that He lives He lives to God (Rom. 6:10).

Who does not need daily, like those high priests, to offer up sacrifices, first for His own sins, and then for the sins of the people, because this He did *once for all* when He offered up Himself (Heb. 7:27)

Nor was it that He should offer Himself often...otherwise He would have needed to suffer often since the foundation of the world; but now *once* at the consummation of the ages he has been manifested to put away sin by the sacrifice of Himself (Heb. 9:25–26).

By this will we have been sanctified through the offering of the body of Jesus Christ *once for all* (Heb. 10:10).

Repeatedly this once–for–all aspect of the work of Christ is emphasized in scripture. The Greek word translated once–for–all is *ephapax*. It is used in particular with reference to Jesus' death and communicates the thought that Christ's death is a finished work which cannot be repeated or perpetuated. It was a unique historic event which is completed and therefore he can never experience death again. In addition to Paul's affirmation of this, Jesus himself states: 'I was dead, and behold, I am alive forevermore' (Rev. 1:18). The word used to describe the death of Jesus as a finished work—*ephapax*—is the same word used to describe his sacrifice and the offering of his body (Heb. 10:10; 9:25–26). Just as Christ cannot die again, neither can his body be offered again or his sacrifice be continued for sin. This is because apart from his death there is no sacrifice that is propitiatory for sin. What made his sacrifice propitiatory in God's eyes was his death. Hebrews 9:22 makes this point: 'Without the shedding of blood there is no forgiveness.' As a result then of this one sacrifice, the bible teaches that God has accomplished a sufficient and finished atonement. On the basis of that finished work God now offers complete and total forgiveness to man. There is no more sacrifice for sin: 'Where there is forgiveness of these things there is no longer any offering for sin' (Heb. 10:18). And since there is no need for further sacrifice, scripture also teaches that there is no need for a continuing sacerdotal priesthood. Christ has fulfilled the Old Testament ceremonial law and it is now abrogated (Heb. 7:11–19). He has become our Sacrifice and Priest and the only Mediator by which we approach God (1 Tim. 2:5; Heb. 7:22–25). Christ's atonement has completely removed the guilt of our sin and its condemnation because he has paid the penalty in full. This will become more evident as we examine the different Greek words used to describe the work of Christ in relationship to sin.

Luo

The Greek word *luo* means to loose. It is found in the famous Matthew 16 passage where Jesus entrusts the keys of the kingdom to Peter and tells him that whatever he binds on earth will be bound in heaven and whatever he looses on earth will be loosed in heaven. *Luo* means to release, to set free, to dissolve or to destroy. Jesus used this word to describe His impending death and resurrection: '*Destroy* this temple and in three days I will raise it up' (Jn. 2:19). Peter uses the word to describe the destruction of the physical universe at the end of the age:

> But the day of the Lord will come like a thief in which the heavens will pass away with a roar and the elements will be *destroyed* with intense heat and the earth and all its works will be burned up. Since these things are to be *destroyed* in this way what sort of people ought we to be in holy conduct and godliness (2 Pet. 3:10–11).

The significance of this word *luo* in the context of salvation is that it is the root word for all Greek words that refer to redemption. For example the word *apolutrosis* is the common Greek word for redemption. It is the word used in Ephesians 1:7: 'In Him we have *redemption* through His blood, the forgiveness of our trespasses.' The word *lutron* which forms part of the word *apolutrosis* means a ransom price. This is the word used by Jesus to describe the meaning of his sacrificial death: 'The Son of Man came not to be served but to serve and to give His life a *ransom* for many' (Mk. 10:45). The word *lutroo* is the verb form of *lutron* and it means to redeem through the payment of a ransom price. Peter describes this in the following words:

> Knowing that you were not *redeemed* with perishable things like silver or gold from your futile way of life inherited from your forefathers, but with precious blood, as of a lamb

unblemished and spotless, the blood of Christ (1 Pet. 1:18–19).

Because a ransom price has been paid (the life of the Lord Jesus given in death) sin has been destroyed and those who are united to Christ are redeemed. They have been set free from sin, and their redemption is eternal:

> To Him who loves us and *released* (loosed) us from our sins by His blood (Rev. 1:5).
>
> But when Christ appeared as a high priest of the good things to come, He entered through the greater and more perfect tabernacle, not made with hands, that is to say, not of this creation; and not through the blood of goats and calves, but through His own blood, He entered the holy place once for all, having obtained *eternal redemption* (Heb. 9:11–12).

Those who are united to Christ possess this redemption. It means a complete and full deliverance from the guilt and condemnation of sin as well as from its bondage. The redeemed in Christ are *loosed* from their sins—cleansed, forgiven and set free—for all eternity:

> As far as the east is from the west, so far has He removed our transgressions from us (Ps. 103:12).

> There is therefore now no condemnation for those who are in Christ Jesus (Rom. 8:1).

> Truly, truly, I say to you, he who hears My word, and believes Him who sent Me, has eternal life, and does not come into judgment, but has passed out of death into life (Jn. 5:24).

> My sheep hear My voice, and I know them, and they follow Me; and I give eternal life to them, and they shall never perish; and no one shall snatch them out of My hand. My Father, who has given them to Me is greater than all; and no

one is able to snatch them out of the Father's hand (Jn. 10:27–29).

When Jesus says that whoever enters into a relationship with him will never enter into judgment he uses the Greek word *krisis*. This word is used in John 5:24 to describe the activity of Jesus himself as Judge:

> For not even the Father judges anyone, but He has given all judgment to the Son...and He gave Him authority to execute judgment because He is the Son of Man. Do not marvel at this; for an hour is coming, in which all who are in the tombs shall hear His voice, and shall come forth; those who did the good deeds to a resurrection of life, those who committed evil deeds to a resurrection of judgment (Jn. 5:22, 27-29; Cf. Mt. 12:36; 1 Tim. 5:24; Heb. 9:27).

Those who have experienced redemption—the loosing of their sins as a result of the work of Jesus in atonement—will never enter into judgment by God for their sins. This is because their sins have already been judged in Jesus.

Aphaireo

The word *aphaireo* means to take away or to remove. In Matthew 26:51 it refers to Peter's removal of the ear of the servant of the high priest. This word is used in Hebrews 10:4 to contrast the animal sacrifices of the Old Testament dispensation with Jesus' atonement. The author of Hebrews emphasizes the superiority of Christ's atonement to the Old Testament sacrifice of animals because his sacrifice takes away sin: 'For it is impossible for the blood of bulls and goats to take away sins...But now once at the consummation of the ages He has been manifested to put away sin by the sacrifice of Himself' (Heb. 10:4; 9:26). The one sacrifice of Jesus completely removes or takes away the guilt of our sin with its consequent judgment and condemnation.

Athetesin

Athetesin means to annul or abolish. It is the word used to describe the annulling or setting aside of the Jewish ceremonial law once the sacrifice of Christ had been completed. It is the same word used to describe the effect of Christ's sacrifice for sin:

> Nor was it that He should offer Himself often, as the high priest enters the holy place year by year with blood not his own. Otherwise He would have needed to suffer often since the foundation of the world; but now once at the consummation of the ages He has been manifested to *put away* sin by the sacrifice of Himself (Heb. 9:26).

By this one sacrifice sin has been annulled, abolished, done away with. As a result, the promise of the New Covenant is that God no longer remembers our sin:

> Their sins and their lawless deeds I will remember no more (Heb. 10:17).

Katherismos

The word *katherismos* means cleansing or purification. It is the word employed by the writer of Hebrews when he refers to Christ's work as a purification from sin: 'When He had made *purification* of sins, He sat down at the right hand of the Majesty on high' (Heb. 1:3). The term is used in the aorist tense here and it speaks of a once–for–all finished work by which Christ has made a complete cleansing of sin. This same word is used in Acts 15:9 by the apostle Peter when he testified to the conversion of the Gentiles: 'And He made no distinction between us and them, cleansing their hearts by faith.' When Peter preached the gospel and the Gentiles responded by trusting in Christ they experienced an instantaneous cleansing of their hearts from sin. It is also the word used by the apostle John in his first epistle where he states that it is the blood of Christ—his finished work of atonement—which is the effectual cause of cleansing from sin's defilement: 'The blood of Jesus His Son cleanses us from all sin' (1 Jn. 1:7). This is true of all who believe savingly in Christ. By faith we experience a complete cleansing from sin through the atonement of Jesus Christ.

Aphesis

Aphesis means forgiveness as it relates to redemption and the ransom price of Christ's sacrifice. The death (blood) of Jesus is the only sufficient payment for our sin. It alone satisfies the justice of God. Scripture teaches that 'all things are cleansed with blood and without the shedding of blood there is no forgiveness' (Heb. 9:22). Since Jesus has shed his blood we have a complete forgiveness through him:

> In Him we have redemption through His blood, the *forgiveness* of our trespasses (Eph. 1:7).
> In whom we have redemption, the *forgiveness* of sins (Col 1:14).
> Now where there is *forgiveness* of these things there are no more sacrifices (Heb. 10:18).

Exalaisas

Exalaisas means to wipe away, to obliterate, to erase, to blot out. It describes what God does with the totality of our sin in Christ:

> He made you alive together with Him, having forgiven us all our transgressions, having *canceled out* the certificate of debt consisting of decrees against us and which was hostile to us; and He has taken it out of the way, having nailed it to the cross (Col. 2:13-14).

Repent therefore and return, that your sins may be *wiped away*, in order that the times of refreshing may come from the presence of the Lord (Acts 3:19).

How many of our sins has Christ died for? Since he died for us before we were even born he died for *all* our sin, not just a portion of it. The certificate of debt consisting of decrees against us—our individual transgressions of the law—has been abolished. It has been nailed to the cross. All our transgressions have been dealt with in Christ. Our debt is completely paid and we are set free. In the mind of God all our transgressions have been canceled out and wiped away because the judgment due them was inflicted upon the Lord Jesus Christ and as a result 'there is therefore now no condemnation for those who are in Christ Jesus' (Rom. 8:1). The Reformation understanding of justification as comprising freedom from the condemnation of the law through the atonement of Christ is expressed by Huldrych Zwingli:

> A second kind of freedom from the Law is that the Law cannot condemn any more, which yet before wrought the wrath and indignation and just vengeance of God, Rom. 4:15 and Gal. 3:10; and Deut. 27:26, where divine justice sternly thunders: 'Cursed is everyone who continueth not in all things that are written in the book of the law, to do them.'
>
> Christ, therefore 'redeemed us from this curse of the law, being made a curse for us,' that is, being nailed to the cross for us, Gal. 3:13 and Rom. 6:10. We are no longer under the Law but under grace; and if under grace, the Law cannot condemn us, for if the Law still has the power to condemn, we are not under grace. It is, therefore, Christ who has broken the wrath of the Law (that is, who has appeased God's justice, which would have caused Him deservedly to rage against us), and who by bearing the cruelty of the cross for us has so softened it that He has chosen to make us not only free instead of slaves, but even sons.. .We are freed from the vengeance of the Law; for Christ has paid by His suffering that penalty

which we owed for our sins. Indeed, we have been so completely freed from sin, as far as it is a disease, that it is no longer able to harm us if we trust in Christ. For 'there is no condemnation to them that are in Christ Jesus, who walk not after the flesh' (Rom. 8:1).[20]

The Reformed understanding of the forensic nature of the atonement of Christ is further elaborated by James Buchanan:

> If we seek to ascertain the reasons which rendered it (Christ's death) necessary...we are taught by Scripture to ascribe it to the sins of men—and the justice of God—viewed in connection with His purpose of saving sinners, in a way consistent with the honour of His law, and the interests of His righteous government, through a Divine Redeemer.
>
> If this be the correct view of the reason of His death...then we cannot fail to regard all the sufferings, which constituted so important a part of Christ's Mediatorial work, as strictly penal. They were the punishment, not of personal, but of imputed, guilt. They were inflicted on Him as the Substitute of sinners. He was 'made a curse' for them, but only because He had been 'made sin for them.' In this view, His sufferings were penal, because they were judicially imposed on Him as the legal representative of those who had come under 'the curse,' according to the rule of that law which proclaimed that 'the wages of sin is death,' and that 'the soul which sinneth it shall die.'[21]

The Atonement and Justification

The atonement is not an on going process. It is a once–for–all, non–repeatable and finished work. This means then that justification is a once–for–all, non–repeatable, finished work. It likewise is not a process. It is an eternal *state* of forgiveness and acceptance with God. Because the atonement is forensic (legal) in nature, justification is also a forensic work. When a man is justified all legal claims against him have been satisfied and he is forgiven. This is in part revealed by the resurrection:

> He was delivered up because of our transgressions and raised because of our justification (Rom. 4:25).

We are told that we possess the *righteousness of God* in justification and that through *this* righteousness we are given an eternal standing of forgiveness and acceptance before him. This is the basis upon which justification becomes a reality for sinful men and women and is the defining issue for a proper understanding of this great biblical doctrine.

The Righteousness of God

Because of God's holiness man needs a righteousness that will truly justify him before God. Such a righteousness must be the perfect fulfilment of his law. The wonderful news of the gospel is that when a man is united to Jesus Christ he is given that righteousness as a gift, the *righteousness of God,* a righteousness which fully satisfies the justice of God and secures for the believer an eternal standing of acceptance and forgiveness before him. But what is the righteousness of God? Is it a righteousness that man is responsible for producing, partially or wholly, or is it a righteousness accomplished completely apart from man's activity, given solely as a gift? It is imperative that we understand the biblical teaching on this matter. If this truth is distorted then the biblical meaning of justification will be distorted with tragic and eternal consequences.

There are at least five different meanings for the word righteousness in the New Testament. Firstly, it describes an attribute of God. God is described as being perfectly righteous in his essential nature (Deut. 32:4). Secondly, it describes the character of Christ as 'Jesus Christ the righteous' (1 Jn. 2:1), meaning that he likewise is perfect and sinless in nature and character. Thirdly, it carries an eschatological meaning. In the future kingdom of God following the second coming of the Lord Jesus, all sin will be eradicated (Rev. 21:27). There will be a new heaven and earth in which righteousness dwells (2 Pet. 3:10-13). This again describes a state of perfection. Fourthly, it describes the experience of sanctification. The believer who enters into a salvation experience with the Lord Jesus Christ becomes a slave of righteousness (Rom. 6:1-22). Though imperfect, the prevailing characteristic of his life will be righteousness. Finally, the word righteousness is used to describe the work of Christ in atonement, designated specifically by the phrase *the righteousness of God*. It is this which is the basis for man's justification, separate and distinct from the other descriptions of righteousness given in scripture. The following scriptures define the nature of this justifying righteousness:

> But whatever things were gain to me, those things I have counted as loss for the sake of Christ...in order that I may gain Christ, and be found in Him, not having a righteousness of my own derived from the Law, but that which is through faith in Christ, *the righteousness which comes from God on the basis of faith*, that I may know Him (Phil 3:7–10).

> He made Him who knew no sin to be sin on our behalf, that *we might become the righteousness of God in Him* (2 Cor. 5:21).

> But now *apart from the Law the righteousness of God has been manifested*, being witnessed by the Law and the Prophets, even *the righteousness of God through faith in Jesus Christ* for all those who believe...being justified as a gift by His grace through the redemption which is in Christ Jesus; whom God displayed publicly as a propitiation in His blood through faith. This was *to demonstrate His righteousness*, because in the forbearance of God He passed over the sins previously committed; *for the demonstration, I say, of His righteousness at the present time*, that He might be just and justifier of the one who has faith in Jesus (Rom. 3:21–26).

Now *to the one who does not work, but believes in Him who justifies the ungodly, his faith is reckoned as righteousness*, just as David also speaks of the blessing upon the man to whom *God reckons righteousness apart from works*: Blessed are those whose lawless deeds have been forgiven, and whose sins have been covered. Blessed is the man whose sin the Lord will not take into account (Rom. 4:4–8).

For if by the transgression of the one death reigned through the one, much more those who receive the abundance of grace and of *the gift of righteousness* will reign in life through the One, Jesus Christ. So then as through one transgression there resulted condemnation to all men, even so *through one act of righteousness there resulted justification of life to all men.* For as through the one man's disobedience the many were made sinners, even so *through the obedience of the One the many will be made righteousness* (Rom. 5:17–19).

Brethren, my heart's desire and my prayer to God for them is for their salvation. For I bear them witness that they have a zeal for God but not according to knowledge. For not knowing about God's righteousness, and seeking to establish their own, they did not subject themselves to *the righteousness of God. For Christ is the end of the law for righteousness to everyone who believes* (Rom. 10:1–4).

But by His doing you are *in Christ Jesus, who became to us* wisdom from God, and *righteousness* and sanctification and redemption (1 Cor. 1:30).

There are a number of key points in these passages regarding the righteousness that justifies. The following points summarize its essential characteristics:

- It is a righteousness that comes from God
- It is an objective, completed righteousness
- It is a righteousness accomplished outside of and apart from man
- It is a gift
- It is given apart from works

- It is imputed
- It is given to the ungodly
- It is received by faith
- It is the Person and obedience of Christ in His work of atonement
- It is given as a result of union with Christ

The righteousness that God requires as a fulfillment of his law is provided as a *gift* in his Son Jesus Christ who is the Lord our righteousness (1 Jn. 2:1; Jer. 23:6). Paul describes the righteousness of God in Romans 3 as a righteousness apart from the law but predicted in the law and the prophets. Such prediction can be found in Isaiah 53, for example, where the atonement of Christ for sin is clearly set forth. Paul states that Christ became a propitiation for sin for the demonstration of the righteousness of God that he might be just in justifying sinners. In other words, the mercy and forgiveness he expresses towards sinners in justifying them is in conformity with the righteous demands of the law and with his holy nature because the Christ who justifies is the Christ who gave his life as a payment for sin in fulfilment of the demands of the law. Therefore the righteousness of God is a person, the Lord Jesus Christ, and it is *his* obedience which is the righteousness that justifies, not that of the believer. Paul brings this out in Romans 5:19–20: 'Through one act of righteousness there resulted justification of life to all men...through the obedience of the One the many will be made righteous.' Note that the work of Christ is described as an act of *righteousness*. When this is compared with Paul's statement in Romans 5:9 that we are 'justified by his blood', we see that the righteousness that justifies is not the righteousness of the individual but the righteousness of the person of Christ in his work of atonement. It is the righteousness of Another. It is also important to note that this righteousness is not limited to Christ's work of atonement but includes his entire life of obedience. Christ fulfils the law as man's substitute positively in that he lived a perfect life of obedience and negatively in that he paid its penalty. James Buchanan gives this explanation of the meaning of justifying righteousness and why it is called the righteousness of God:

> If we would understand the reason why it is called 'the righteousness of God,' we must bear in mind that there was a twofold manifestation of righteousness in the Cross of Christ: there was first a manifestation of the righteousness of God the Father, in requiring a satisfaction to His justice, and inflicting the punishment that was due to sin; and to this the Apostle refers when he says, that 'God set forth Christ to be a propitiation'—'to declare His righteousness, that He might be just, and the Justifier of him that believeth in Jesus;' there was, secondly, a work of righteousness by God the Son—His vicarious righteousness as the Redeemer of His people... 'This is the name whereby He shall be called, The Lord our righteousness' (Jer. 23:6). He is so called on account of the righteousness which He wrought out by His obedience unto death; for this righteousness is expressly connected with His Mediatorial work...By His vicarious sufferings and obedience, He fulfilled the Law both in its precept and its penalty; and is now said to be 'the end of the law for righteousness to every one that believeth' (Rom. 10:3–4).[22]

Paul says that this righteousness is given as a gift by faith, to the ungodly, completely apart from works. If it is a righteousness that is given *apart from works* and *to the ungodly*, then it must be independent of human works. It is a *completed* righteousness that is given and received. This is not something that one works to achieve. This is very important in helping us to understand the meaning of justification. Paul's phrase 'apart from works' is another way of stating the Reformation teaching of faith alone. This simply means that there is no work an individual can contribute to his justification.

Some have suggested that when he uses the phrase 'by the works of the law', Paul is not referring to the moral law but to the Jewish ceremonial law. They suggest that while we must repudiate the Jewish ceremonial law as a basis for justification that this is not so for the moral law. However, in the book of Romans, Paul uses the term law to include both the ceremonial and the moral law of God. In Romans 7:7–13 he specifically repudiates the moral law as a basis for justification. Because the righteousness which justifies is a gift of God, justification then is also a gift. The righteousness that justifies us is something completely external to us. This is why the Reformers called it an 'alien righteousness'.

Justification is a forensic (legal) term which deals with acquittal from the claims of the law. It is based upon the atonement of Christ which was offered in the context of legal demands. Again, we see the direct connection between justification and the atonement in Romans 5:9 which states that we are 'justified by His blood.' Justification is a declaration of a righteousness based on the imputation of the righteousness of Christ. Justification does not mean to 'make righteous' morally, but to *declare* to be righteous legally. It has to do with a person's legal status before God the holy Judge. This is the particular meaning the word justification has within the overall context of salvation. It means to be acquitted from guilt, to be set free from condemnation and to be fully accepted by God.

There are two Greek words in the New Testament, both derived from the same root, which are translated by the words righteousness (*dikaiosune*), and justify (*dikaioo*). Thayer's *Greek–English Lexicon of the New Testament* defines *dikaioo* as: 'to declare, pronounce one to be just, righteous, or such as he ought to be; to declare guiltless one accused or who may be accused, acquit of a charge or reproach; to judge, declare, pronounce righteous and therefore acceptable.' The noun *dikaiosune* means: 'The state of him who is such as he ought to be, righteousness; the condition acceptable to God; denotes the state acceptable to God which becomes a sinner's possession through that faith by which he embraces the grace of God offered him in the expiatory death of Christ.' Leon

Morris makes these important observations on the meaning of the word justification as it is used in scripture:

> It is necessary to say a word...about the verb *dikaioo* which in the New Testament is translated 'to justify' but which has been understood in more ways than one. Since verbs in *-ow* commonly express a causative idea it is urged by some that *dikaioo* must mean to 'make righteous'. But it is to be noted in the first place that verbs of this class denoting moral qualities do not have the causative meaning (e.g. *axioo* means 'to deem worthy' not 'to make worthy' and similarly with *homioo, hosioo* etc.), and in the second, that in any case the meaning of a word is to be determined in the last resort by the way people used it. We cannot at this distance in time say that, since a verb is formed in such and such a fashion, therefore the Greeks must have understood it to mean so and so; all that we can do is to note how they did in fact use it, and deduce from that what it meant to them. And by this test *dikaioo* certainly does not mean 'to make righteous.' In Greek literature generally it seems to mean 'to hold right', 'to deem right', and thence 'to claim or demand as a right', and 'to do a man right or justice'...Neither the word structure nor the use of the verb outside the Bible, then, gives countenance to the idea that 'to make righteous' is the meaning we are to understand.
>
> When we turn to those passages where the verb 'to justify' occurs, there can be no doubt that the meaning is to declare rather than to make righteous...the basic idea is one of acquittal...The Hebrew and Greek verbs remind us of processes of law, and take their essential meaning from those processes of law. That a declaratory process rather a making righteous is meant is clear from the fact that the verb is applied to Jehovah (Ps. 51: 4), for it is an impossible thought that He should be 'made righteous' in any sense other than 'made righteous before men' or 'declared righteous'.
>
> When we turn to the noun and the adjective from this root we find the same essentially forensic significance. The

righteous are those acquitted at the bar of God's justice, and righteousness is the standing of those so acquitted.

Nobody who has taken the trouble to examine the ninety-two examples of the use of *dikaiosune* in the New Testament will doubt that the forensic use is primary...When, for example, St. Paul speaks of the righteousness which is by faith, he is not thinking in terms of mercy in men, but of their legal standing before God.[23]

The declarative nature of justification is taught in Romans 5:19 where we read: 'For as through the one man's disobedience the many were made sinners, even so through the obedience of the one the many will be made righteous.' The terms 'made sinners' and 'made righteous' do not refer to our moral condition but to our status or position before God. It refers to a reckoning in the mind of God. Before a man is even born he is reckoned to be a sinner. The word translated 'made' is *kathistemi*. It means to set down as, to constitute, to declare. It is used twenty-two times in the New Testament and in most cases it means to be appointed to some kind of position. Thus, to be justified by the imputed righteousness of Christ is to be reckoned as righteous in God's eyes, to hold the status or position of righteousness, to be acquitted from the condemnation and judgment of the law based on the once-for-all atonement of Christ. God declares that believers have fulfilled the demands of the law *in Christ*. Believers are united with Christ in his death, burial and resurrection so that his experience and standing before God becomes theirs (Rom. 6:1–5). In other words, the believer who is united to Christ is imputed with his righteousness. This actually constitutes him righteous judicially before God because this righteousness is a *real* righteousness. As John Murray observes:

Justification means to declare to be righteous—it is a judgment based upon the recognition that a person stands in right relation to law and justice...How can God justify the ungodly?...God's justification of the ungodly presupposes or comprises within itself—that is to say the action of God denoted by justification of the ungodly—another action *besides that which is expressed by our English word 'declare righteous'*...This action is one in which he actually causes to be the relation which in justification is declared to be. He effects a right relation as well as declares that relation to be. In other words he constitutes the state which is declared to be. Hence the justifying act either includes or presupposes the constitutive act. This alone will make the declaration to be a declaration according to truth...It is not only through the one righteous act (Romans 5:18) but it is by the bestowal of the free gift of righteousness...That is to say justification has not only righteousness as its proper ground, it is not only that God has respect to righteousness, but it is also a bestowment of righteousness and, because so, there is the assurance of life...Now if there is an imputation of righteousness, such righteousness meets the requirement of establishing a new relationship which not only warrants the declaration but elicits and demands it and ensures the acceptance of the person as righteous in God's sight.[24]

In 1 Corinthians 1:30 Paul states, 'But by His doing you are in Christ Jesus *who* became to us wisdom from God and *righteousness* and sanctification and redemption.' Here Paul uses the word righteousness as a synonym for justification and separates justification from sanctification as concepts. Justifying righteousness is a separate concept and work from that of sanctification though they both come under the general heading of salvation. Justification and sanctification are not interchangeable terms in the New Testament. They are two entirely different aspects of the overall work of salvation. Paul maintains that the righteousness that justifies is a person, the Lord Jesus Christ: 'By His doing you are *in Christ Jesus, who* became to us...*righteousness*.' He does not say that Christ is the source of grace by which a person may become righteous through sanctification. He uses the term sanctification for that. When he uses the word *righteousness* with respect to justification, the apostle is underscoring the wonderful truth that in Christ God provides a completed righteousness, apart from the works of man. This righteousness instantly and forever justifies an individual by conferring upon him a legal *state* of eternal righteousness. It is a righteousness which has fulfilled the just demands of the law of God.

Just as man's sin was imputed to Christ, so Christ's righteousness is imputed to the true believer. The whole concept of imputation is essential to the doctrine of justification. This is not the invention of the Protestant Reformers but the express teaching of scripture itself. In Romans 4:5–6 Paul writes: 'But to the one who does not work, but believes in Him who justifies the ungodly, his faith is *reckoned* as righteousness, just as David also speaks of the blessing upon the man to whom God *reckons* righteousness apart from works.' The Greek word translated 'reckon' in these two verses is *logizomai*. It means to 'reckon, count, compute, calculate, count over; hence...to pass to one's account, to impute' (*Thayer's Greek–English Lexicon of the New Testament*). This word is used forty–one times in the New Testament. It means a mental evaluation, conclusion or judgment regarding a particular issue. It is an accounting term. Paul illustrates this in his letter to Philemon when referring to Philemon's former slave Onesimus: 'But if he has wronged you in any way, or owes you anything, charge that to my account' (verse 18). Charge that to my account! In other words, impute that to me. Joel Beeke describes the relationship between justification and imputation:

> Justification is...a sister–concept to imputation. As a forensic (i.e. legal or judicial) term, justification is the act of God's sovereign grace whereby He imputes to the elect sinner, who is in himself guilty and condemned, the perfect righteousness of Christ, acquits him on the ground of Christ's merits of all guilt and punishment, grants him a right to eternal life, and enables him to lay hold of and appropriate to himself Christ

and His benefits. Imputation signifies to credit something to someone's account by transfer, i.e. God transfers the perfect righteousness of Christ to the elect sinner as a gracious gift, and transfers all of the sinner's unrighteousness to Christ who has paid the full price of satisfaction for that unrighteousness. By means of this mutual transfer the justified sinner is viewed by God as if 'he never had had, nor committed any sin,' but had himself 'fully accomplished all that obedience which Christ has accomplished' (*Heidelberg Catechism*, Q. 60; cf. Romans 4:4–6; 5:12–19; 2 Corinthians 5:21).[25]

So the basic thrust of Paul's teaching on imputation in Romans 4 is this: In justification God imputes or credits a completed righteousness, the obedience of Another, to the one who comes by faith alone to Christ. This results in an eternal state of forgiveness and acceptance with God. On the basis of that imputed righteousness God comes to a settled evaluation about the individual—he is judged to be righteous. Historically, the whole concept of imputed righteousness for justification has been mocked by the Roman Catholic Church. She calls it a legal fiction. This is a serious charge. But in labelling this a legal fiction the Roman Catholic Church brings this charge against God himself. If the imputation of Christ's righteousness is fiction then the imputation of our sin to him is also fiction. But the imputation of righteousness is the explicit teaching of scripture. In justification there is a *real* righteousness and a *real* imputation, just as in the atonement Christ bore in *reality* our sin and died a *real* death. This is *not* a legal fiction.

There are today Roman Catholic apologists who repudiate any notion of justification as a forensic concept. For example, in the spring of 1995, CURE (Christians United For Reformation) hosted a debate between Protestants and Roman Catholics on Justification. Robert Sungenis, one of the Roman Catholic participants, made the following comments on justification:

The concept of juridical justification at the initial point of justification has no biblical support. The only thing close to a courtroom scene for salvation is at the end of time when Christ stands as the Judge of all. The biblical context of initial justification has as its New Testament background a relational, familial context. Though it is granted that words for righteousness or justification can etymologically be shown to have some juridical basis, this is primarily in the Old Testament legal theocracy and even then eighty–five to ninety percent of these uses are moral, not juridical.

The main question is, What does faith have to do with jurisprudence? The answer is, nothing. But it has everything to do with relationships. The words legal, forensic, contract, verdict, acquitted, defended, court, courtroom, lawyer, juridical, jury, judge, do not appear in reference to our initial justification with God in the New Testament. *When the New Testament is describing justification or salvation it never uses a courtroom scene.* It uses many other paradigms but not a courtroom. Instead, Abraham is called the friend of God when he is justified, not the acquitted defendent. There is the enemy/friend paradigm (Rom 5, 9 and James 2:23). There is the marriage/widowhood paradigm (Rom. 7:1–4). There is the bondwoman/freewoman paradigm (Gal. 4:21ff). There is the legitimate/illegitimate son paradigm (Heb. 12). There is the Jew/Gentile paradigm (Gal. 2, Eph. 3). And finally there is the adoption paradigm (Rom. 8:15, 23; Rom. 9:4; Eph. 1:5).[26]

In light of the fact that justification is grounded upon the atonement of Christ (which Galatians 3 tells us is performed in the context of the demands of the law of God) these assertions by Robert Sungenis are patently false. To actually suggest that scripture nowhere represents justification in a legal sense is to completely misrepresent the teaching of scripture. The cross of Christ is in fact one big courtroom scene. It is a vindication of the justice of God, as Romans 3 teaches, enabling God to be a just Judge while mercifully justifying sinners. While it is true that in salvation believers are adopted into the family of God, coming to know him as Father, it is equally true that the basis for such a relationship is the satisfaction of the justice of God who is a righteous and holy Judge. The following comments from leading Reformers sum up the Reformation understanding of the meaning of justification based on imputed righteousness and the finished work of Christ in atonement in these words:

John Calvin: Let us explain what these expressions mean: that man is justified in God's sight, and that he is justified by faith or works. He is said to be justified in God's sight who is both reckoned righteous in God's judgment and has been accepted on account of his righteousness. Indeed as iniquity is abominable to God, so no sinner can find favor in his eyes in so far as he is a sinner and so long as he is reckoned as such. Accordingly wherever there is sin, there also the wrath and vengeance of God show themselves. Now he is justified who is reckoned in the condition not of a sinner, but of a righteous man; and for that reason, he stands firm before God's judgment seat while all sinners fall. If an innocent accused person be summoned before the judgment seat of a fair judge, where he will be judged according to his innocence, he is said to be 'justified' before the judge. Thus, justified before God is the man who, freed from the company of sinners, has God to witness and affirm his righteousness. In the same way, therefore, he in whose life that purity and holiness will be found which deserves a testimony of righteousness before God's throne will be said to be justified by works, or else he who, by the wholeness of his works, can meet and satisfy God's judgment. On the contrary, justified by faith is he who, excluded from the righteousness of works, grasps the righteousness of Christ through faith, and clothed in it, appears in God's sight not as a sinner but as a righteous man. Therefore we explain justification simply as the acceptance with which God receives us into his favor as righteous men. And we say that it consists in the remission of sins and the imputation of Christ's righteousness.

Therefore, 'to justify' means nothing else than to acquit of guilt him who was accused, as if his innocence were confirmed. Therefore, since God justifies us by the intercession of Christ, he absolves us not by the confirmation of our innocence but by the imputation of righteousness, so that we who are not righteous in ourselves may be reckoned as such in Christ.[27]

Martin Luther: Because an eternal, unchangeable sentence of condemnation has passed upon sin—for God cannot and will not regard sin with favor, but his wrath abides upon it eternally and irrevocably—redemption was not possible without a ransom of such precious worth as to atone for sin, to assume the guilt, pay the price of wrath and thus abolish sin.

This no creature was able to do. There was no remedy except for God's only Son to step into our distress and himself become man, to take upon himself the load of awful and eternal wrath and make his own body and blood a sacrifice for sin. And so he did, out of the immeasurably great mercy and love towards us, giving himself up and bearing the sentence of unending wrath and death.

So infinitely precious to God is this sacrifice and atonement of his only begotten Son who is one with him in divinity and majesty, that God is reconciled thereby and receives into grace and forgiveness of sins all who believe in his Son. Only by believing may we enjoy the precious atonement of Christ, the forgiveness obtained for us and given us out of profound, inexpressible love. We have nothing to boast of for ourselves, but must ever joyfully thank and praise him who at such priceless cost redeemed us condemned and lost sinners.[28]

Thomas Cranmer: It is our part and duty ever to remember the great mercy of God; how that, all the world being wrapped in sin by breaking of the law, God sent his only Son our Saviour Christ into this world to fulfil the law for us; and by shedding his most precious blood, to make a sacrifice and satisfaction, or (as it may be called) amends, to his Father for our sins, to asuage his wrath and indignation conceived against us for the same...In our justification is not only God's mercy and grace, but also his justice, which the apostle calls 'the justice of God'; and it consisteth in paying our ransom and fulfilling the law. And so the grace of God doth not exclude the justice of God in our justification, but only excludeth the justice of man, that is to say, the justice of our works, as to be merits deserving of our justification...It pleased our heavenly Father, of his infinite mercy, without any our desert or deserving, to prepare for us the most precious jewels of Christ's body and blood, whereby our ransom might be fully paid, the law fulfilled, and his justice fully satisfied. So that Christ is now the righteousness of them that truly do believe in him. He for them paid their ransom by his death. He for them fulfilled the law in his life. So that now in him and by him every true Christian man may be called a fulfiller of the law; forasmuch as that which their infirmity lacketh, Christ's justice hath supplied.[29]

The judicial basis of our relationship with God is also seen in the New Testament teaching on the New Covenant. The New Covenant is a term used to describe the new relationship with God that is effected for man through the person and work of Jesus Christ. The whole concept of covenant is at the heart of God's revelation to man. The New Testament is but a record of the fulfilment and continuation of the Abrahamic covenant of the Old Testament (Rom. 4:1–4; Gal. 3:6–29). In this Covenant God brings man into a new relationship with himself in which man experiences forgiveness of sins, an experiential knowledge of God and a new heart sanctified unto God. This covenant is mediated through the person of Jesus Christ on the basis of his once–for–all atonement for sin. The New Testament frequently speaks of the 'blood of the covenant.' For example, Hebrews 9:15 states: 'And for this reason He is the mediator of a new covenant, in order that since a death has taken place for the redemption of the transgressions that were committed under the first covenant, those who have been called may receive the promise of eternal life.' And Jesus, when he initiated the Lord's Supper as a memorial of his sacrificial death, put it in covenantal terms when he said: 'This is My blood of the covenant, which is poured out for many for the forgiveness of sins...This cup which is poured out for you is the new covenant in My blood' (Mt. 26:28; Lk. 22:20). These passages and others make it clear that apart from Christ's death, given as a payment for sin in atonement to God, there would be no new covenant, no New Testament dispensation. The whole basis for our relationship with God is legal in nature because it is grounded solidly upon the atonement of the Lord Jesus Christ.

Grace and Faith

To understand imputed righteousness is to understand grace and faith. Grace is the means by which everything necessary for man to receive forgiveness and eternal acceptance has been provided as a gift by God through the work of his Son. It is not a work achieved or merited by man in any way. It is accomplished by Christ *alone*. It is *his* righteousness, not man's. Therefore from a biblical standpoint, grace alone means by Christ *alone,* received by faith *alone* and not by works. As Paul puts it:

> If it is by grace it is no longer on the basis of works otherwise grace is no longer grace (Rom. 11:6).
> For we maintain that a man is justified by faith apart from the works of the Law (Rom. 3:28).

Repeatedly, scripture tells us that justification is not by works, either before or after a person has come into the experience of grace. For example Titus 3:5 states: 'He saved us, not on the basis of deeds which we have done in righteousness, but according to His mercy.' Paul states that works are not the basis for our salvation, grace empowered or otherwise. Why is this so? Because Christ has done all the work necessary for justification:

> By grace you have been saved through faith; and that not of yourselves, it is the gift of God; not as a result of works, that no one should boast (Eph. 2:8–9).

Some Roman Catholic apologists point out that the verb form for justify is found in the aorist, present and future tenses in the New Testament. They maintain this proves that justification is not a completed work but an ongoing process which is dependent upon the human works of sanctification. However such assertions are laid to rest by Galatians 2:16 where all three verb tenses are found in relation to justification:

> Nevertheless knowing that a man is not justified (present) by the works of the Law but through faith in Christ Jesus, even we have believed in Christ Jesus, that we may be justified (aorist) by faith in Christ and not by the works of the Law; since by the works of the Law shall no flesh be justified (future).

Paul states emphatically that no man is ever justified by works, whether it be the past, present or future. He is writing to the Galatians who have already experienced the grace of God. He is warning these believers that justification is not a process based upon human works, even works in cooperation with grace, but solely upon faith in Christ at a point in time. Paul makes it clear in this same letter that if a gospel of justification by works is preached it will result in the corrupting and distorting of the true gospel of grace:

> I am amazed that you are so quickly deserting Him who called you by the grace of Christ, for another gospel; which is really not another; only there are some who are disturbing you, and want to distort the gospel of Christ. But even though we, or an

angel from heaven, should preach to you a gospel contrary to that which we have preached to you, let him be accursed. As we have said before, so I say again now, if any man is preaching to you a gospel contrary to that which you received, let him be accursed (Gal. 1:6–9).

Works as a *basis* for justification must be repudiated and an exclusive trust in and reliance upon the person of Christ and his work of atonement alone for salvation must be exercised if one is to have saving faith. This is the Reformation truth of *sola fide* or faith alone. It is another way of stating the truth of Romans 3:28: 'For we maintain that a man is justified by faith *apart from the works of the Law.'*

The Place of Works

Is there any place for works? The bible answers in the affirmative. In the book of James we read:

What use is it, my brethren, if a man says he has faith, but he has no works? Can that faith save him? If a brother or sister is without clothing and in need of daily food, and one of you says to them, 'Go in peace, be warmed and be filled,' and yet you do not give them what is necessary for their body, what use is that? Even so faith, if it has no works, is dead being by itself.

But someone may well say, 'You have faith, and I have works; show me your faith without the works, and I will show you my faith by my works.' You believe that God is one. You do well; the demons also believe and shudder. But are you willing to recognize, you foolish fellow, that faith without works is useless? Was not Abraham our father justified by works, when he offered up Isaac his son on the altar? You see that faith was working with his works, and as a result of the works, faith was perfected; and the Scripture was fulfilled which says, 'And Abraham believed God and it was reckoned to him as righteousness,' and he was called the friend of God.

You see that a man is justified by works, and not by faith alone.

In light of Paul's teaching on justification by faith how are we to understand James? Was Abraham justified by works in addition to faith? Does this support the Roman Catholic position that justification should include works? To interpret James properly there are a number of important principles to keep in mind. In Romans, Paul deals with the nature of justification. In James the issue is the nature or character of saving faith. James addresses the issue of dead faith, as opposed to living, saving faith. Dead faith is 'faith' that makes a profession but it has no effect on the life, what many call today, easy–believism, dead orthodoxy or mere intellectual assent. Dead faith produces no fruit, no accompanying works to testify to the veracity or reality of the professed faith—put simply, no holiness. So while Paul deals with the issue of legalism as it relates to justification, James deals with antinomianism as it relates to faith.

The key phrase in James 2 is 'show me your faith' (Js. 2:18). The only way true saving faith is demonstrated is through works. 'Show me your faith without the works, and I will show you my faith by my works' (Js. 2:18). True saving faith will always be demonstrated or accompanied by works of love and holiness. According to Romans 4:2 Abraham was justified by faith apart from works. He was declared righteous by God. But how do we know he truly had saving faith? Because his works revealed and vindicated his faith before men. His faith bore the fruit of love for God. In that sense his works justified his faith. Faith alone justifies but the faith that justifies will always give evidence of its existence, bearing fruit in holiness of life. In Matthew 11:19 we are told, 'Wisdom is vindicated (justified)by her deeds.' The word for vindicated here is the Greek word justify. It simply means that wisdom is revealed or demonstrated as true wisdom by the evidence of its works. The works do not make it wisdom. Wisdom exists, but the works reveal its existence. It is the same with true saving faith.

Justification and faith already exist but the reality of saving faith is always evidenced by works. The *Dictionary of New Testament Theology* puts it this way: 'In the expression, faith working through love (Gal. 5:16), love is specified as the means by which faith becomes visibly operative or effective.'[30] This is further amplified by the apostle John in his first epistle. John states, 'By *this* we know that we have come to know Him, if we keep His commandments...no one who is born of God practices sin, for His seed abides in him; and he cannot sin because he is born of God' (1 Jn. 2:3; 3:9). John is teaching that a righteous life is the *evidence* of the new birth. If an individual is truly united to Jesus Christ he will give evidence to that reality by living a righteous life. The works of righteousness do not produce the new birth or the knowledge of God, rather they give evidence of it. Jesus teaches the same truth. In John 15:8 he says, 'By this is My Father glorified, that you bear much fruit, and so *prove* to be My disciples' (Jn. 15:8). The fruit of righteousness gives evidence or proof that one has come into a saving relationship with Jesus Christ. The disciple relationship already exists and the works are evidence of the reality of that relationship. Likewise Jesus disabuses the Pharisees of the notion that they were the children of Abraham when he states that if they were, they would do the deeds of Abraham (Jn. 8:39). Instead they give evidence of the fact that they are the children of Satan (Jn. 8:44). He says that if God were truly their Father they would love him (Jn. 8:42). In other words, a person's true nature is revealed by his attitudes and life. The deeds do not create the nature but reveal its existence. Jesus teaches that a tree is known by its fruit (Mt. 7:16–20). The fruit does not create the tree but reveals the type of tree it is. Similarly, a righteous life is the obvious and inevitable result of true salvation. It is the *fruit* of union with Christ. This same truth is expressed by Paul when he says, 'Therefore, my brethren, you also were made to die to the Law through the body of Christ, that you might be joined to another, to Him who was raised from the dead, that we might bear fruit for God' (Rom. 7:4). First comes the relationship with Christ and then follows the fruit as an evidence of the union. After stating in Ephesians 2:8–9 that salvation is not by works, Paul goes on to say: 'For we are His workmanship, created in Christ Jesus for good works, which God prepared beforehand, that we should walk in them' (Eph. 2:10). Though works are not the basis for our salvation, we are saved to bring forth works which glorify God. Philip Melanchthon, the Reformer and close friend and associate of Martin Luther, makes these comments on the relationship between faith and works:

> Paul is here (1 Corinthians 12–13)...demanding love in addition to faith. This is what he does elsewhere in all his letters, demanding good works from believers, i.e. the justified...And when he says that he who has all faith but no love is nothing, he is right. For although faith alone justifies, love is also demanded...But love does not justify because no one loves as he ought. Faith, however, justifies...There is also the passage in James 2:17: 'So faith by itself, if it has no works, is dead.' He did well to say this, for he was reprimanding those who thought that faith is merely a historical opinion about Christ. For just as Paul calls one type of faith 'true,' and the other 'feigned,' so James calls the one kind 'living' and the other 'dead.' A living faith is that efficacious, burning trust in the mercy of God which never fails to bring forth good fruits. That is what James says in ch. 2:22: 'Faith was completed by works.'...Therefore, the whole point that James is making is that dead faith...does not justify, but a living faith justifies. But a living faith is that which pours itself out in works. For he speaks as follows (v. 18): 'Show me your faith apart from your works, and I by my works will show you my faith.' But he does not say: 'I will show you works without faith.' My exposition squares most harmoniously with what we read in James: 'So faith by itself, if it has no works, is dead.' Therefore, it is obvious that he is teaching here merely that faith is dead in those who do not bring forth the fruit of faith, even though from external appearances they seem to believe.[31]

Thomas Cranmer, expresses a similar view:

> The first entry unto God, good Christian people, is through faith; whereby...we be justified before God. And, lest any man should be deceived for lack of right understanding thereof, it is diligently to be noted that faith is taken in the Scripture two manner of ways. There is one faith which in Scripture is called a dead faith, which bringeth forth no good works, but is idle, barren, and unfruitful. And this faith by the holy apostle St. James is compared to the faith of devils, which believe God to be true and just, and tremble for fear, yet they do nothing well, but all evil. And such manner of faith have the wicked and naughty Christian people; 'which confess God,' as St. Paul saith, 'in their mouth, but deny him in their deeds, being abominable and without the right faith and in all good works reprovable...This dead faith therefore is not that sure and substantial faith which saveth sinners...The true, lively, and unfeigned Christian faith...is not in the mouth and outward profession only, but it liveth, and stirreth inwardly in the heart. And this faith is not without hope and trust in God, nor without the love of God and of our neighbours, nor without the fear of God, nor without the desire to hear God's word, and to follow the same in eschewing evil and doing gladly all good works.[32]

Sanctification cannot be separated from justification in the overall experience of salvation. When an individual is justified he begins the process of growth in holiness called sanctification or fruitbearing. The bible teaches nothing of justification without sanctification. If there is no fruit, then as James says, the professed faith is dead and will not save. A faith that lacks the fruit of obedience is nothing more than intellectual assent and therefore, dead orthodoxy.

Paul states, 'There will be tribulation and distress for every soul of man who does evil, of the Jew first and also of the Greek, but glory and honor and peace to every man who does good, to the Jew first and also to the Greek' (Rom. 2:9–10).

And Jesus said, 'Do not marvel at this; for an hour is coming, in which all who are in the tombs shall hear His voice, and shall come forth; those who did the good deeds to a resurrection of life, those who committed the evil deeds to a resurrection of judgment' (Jn. 5:28–29). Jesus and Paul are not teaching salvation by works. Rather, they are stressing the necessity of works as the evidence of saving faith, the visible criteria by which a true relationship with Christ is judged to exist. It is the relationship, not works, which *is* the basis for entrance into the kingdom of God.

What about rewards? This issue was a point of contention between the Reformers and Rome due to Rome's theology of merit. Roman Catholicism consistently misinterprets scripture regarding rewards by equating them with eternal life. For example, Roman Catholic theologian, Ludwig Ott, states:

> According to Holy Writ, eternal blessedness in heaven is the reward...for good works performed on this earth...Jesus promises rich rewards in Heaven to those, who for His sake are scorned and persecuted: 'Be glad and rejoice, for your reward is very great in heaven' (Mt. 5:12). The judge of the world decrees eternal reward for the just on the ground of their good works: 'Come, ye blessed of my Father, possess you the kingdom prepared for you from the foundation of the world. For I was hungry and you gave me to eat (Mt. 25:34). In Christ's discourses the reward motive frequently recurs.[33]

It is clear from the teaching of Jesus that he does promise rewards for faithful service. For example he states: 'For whoever gives you a cup of water to drink because of your name as followers of Christ, truly I say to you, he shall not lose his reward' (Mt. 9:41). In another place he says: 'Blessed are you when men cast insults at you, and persecute you, and say all kinds of evil against you falsely, on account of Me. Rejoice, and be glad, for your reward in heaven is great, for so they persecuted the prophets who were before you' (Mt. 5:11–12). Note, however, that the rewards spoken of here are not heaven or eternal life. As we have seen, eternal life is a free gift (Rom. 6:23). It cannot be earned or merited by human works. Rewards on the other hand are for faithful, persevering service. John Murray helps us to understand the relationship between justification and works and rewards:

> While it makes void the gospel to introduce works in connection with justification, nevertheless works done in faith, from the motive of love to God, in obedience to the revealed will of God and to the end of his glory are intrinsically good and acceptable to God. As such they will be the criterion of reward in the life to come. This is apparent from such passages as Matthew 10:41; 1 Corinthians 3:8–9, 11–15; 4:5; 2 Corinthians 5:10; 2 Timothy 4:7. We must maintain therefore, justification complete and irrevocable by grace through faith and apart from works, and at the same time, future reward according to works. In reference to these two doctrines it is important to observe the following: (i) This future reward is not justification and contributes nothing to that which constitutes justification. (ii) This future reward is not salvation. Salvation is by grace and it is not a reward for works that we are saved. (iii) The reward has reference to the station a person is to occupy in glory and does not have reference to the gift of glory itself. While the reward is of grace yet the standard or criterion of judgment by which the degree of reward is to be determined is good works. (iv) This reward is not administered because good works earn or merit reward, but because God is graciously pleased to reward them. That is to say it is a reward of grace. In the Romish scheme good works have real merit and constitute the ground of the title to everlasting life. The good works are rewarded because they are intrinsically good and well–pleasing to God. They are not rewarded because they earn reward but they are rewarded only as labour, work or service that is the fruit of God's grace, conformed to his will and therefore intrinsically good and well–pleasing to him. They could never be rewarded of grace if they were principally and intrinsically

evil.[34]

Works do not save or justify. But a saved life will demonstrate itself in a life of sanctification and faithful service to the Lord. This was the consistent teaching of the Reformers and all those who are true to their teaching. In teaching faith alone neither Calvin or Luther ever implied that one could be justified and yet go on living in sin. They taught what scripture teaches: that when an individual is saved he is eternally justified, but also regenerated, sanctified and adopted. Justification is but one aspect of the overall work of salvation, as is sanctification. Although both doctrines come under the general heading of salvation they are not interchangeable terms. They are separate blessings which flow simultaneously from union with Christ. The Protestant Reformers affirmed the biblical teaching of imputed righteousness for justification as well as, and in addition to, the necessity for regeneration and the indwelling of the Holy Spirit for sanctification, but without confusing the terms. They consistently taught that justification is by faith alone but by a faith evidenced by or which necessitates the works of sanctification. So the emphasis of the Reformation was upon a twofold understanding of righteousness. Firstly, in justification there is the imputation of the righteousness of Christ and secondly, by the indwelling of the Holy Spirit, there is the living out of the righteousness of sanctification. This is well expressed, for example, by Martin Luther:

> Through faith in Christ, therefore, Christ's righteousness becomes our righteousness and all that he has becomes ours; rather, he himself becomes ours. Therefore the Apostle calls it 'the righteousness of God.' in Rom. 1:17: For in the gospel 'the righteousness of God is revealed...as it is written, "The righteousness man shall live by faith." '...This is an infinite righteousness, and one that swallows up all sin in a moment, for it is impossible that sin should exist in Christ. On the contrary, he who trusts in Christ exists in Christ; he is one

with Christ, having the same righteousness as he...Therefore this alien righteousness, instilled in us without our works by grace alone—while the Father, to be sure, inwardly draws us to Christ—is set opposite original sin, likewise alien, which we acquire without our works by birth alone.

The second kind of righteousness is our proper righteousness, not because we alone work it, but because we work with that first and alien righteousness. This is the manner of life spent profitably in good works, in the first place, in slaying the flesh and crucifying the desires with respect to the self, of which we read in Gal. 5:24: 'And those who belong to Christ Jesus have crucified the flesh with its passions and desires.' In the second place, this righteousness consists in love to one's neighbor, and in the third place, in meekness and fear toward God...This righteousness is the product of the righteousness of the first type, actually its fruit and consequence...This righteousness goes on to complete the first for it ever strives to do away with the old Adam and to destroy the body of sin. Therefore it hates itself and loves its neighbor; it does not seek its own good, but that of another, and this its whole way of living consists. For in that it hates itself and does not seek its own, it crucifies the flesh. Because it seeks the good of another, it works love. Thus in each sphere it does God's will, living soberly with self, justly with neighbor, devoutly toward God.[35]

The English Reformer, John Hooper, says:

It is no profit to say sole faith justifieth, except godliness of life follow, as Paul saith: 'If ye live according to the flesh, ye shall die.[36]

Thus, while the Reformation teaching of faith alone (*sola fide*) means a repudiation of all works as necessary for justification, it is not a repudiation of works in general. The Reformers unanimously insisted on the necessity for the works of sanctification.

The Results of Justification

Justification is an eternal declaration of God which happens the moment an individual is united to Christ. It is not a process dependent upon the works of an individual but an instantaneous act of God. The sinner is translated out of a *state* of sin and enmity with God into a *state* of forgiveness and acceptance with him. He is reconciled to and has peace with God (Rom. 5:1). He is set free from all judgment and condemnation (Rom. 8:1). The believer is brought into a filial relationship with God through the New Covenant. He is adopted—made a child of God (Rom. 8:15–17; Eph. 1:5; 1 Jn. 3:1–2). It is not uncommon in the polemics between Protestantism and Roman Catholicism for Roman Catholics to misrepresent the true teaching of the Reformation. All too often Roman apologists give the impression that imputed righteousness in justification is the totality of the Protestant teaching on salvation—that it includes nothing more. There is rarely any mention made that the true position of the Reformation is an affirmation not only of imputed righteousness for justification but also of sanctification, regeneration and adoption. Even a cursory reading of Reformed theology reveals this to be the case. For example, with respect to the teaching of adoption the Westminster Confession states:

> All those that are justified, God vouchsafeth, in and for his only Son Jesus Christ, to make partakers of the grace of adoption: by which they are taken into the number, and enjoy the liberties and privileges of the children of God; have his name put upon them, receive the Spirit of adoption; have access to the throne of grace with boldness; are enabled to cry, Abba, Father; are pitied, protected, provided for, and chastened by him as a father; yet never cast off, but sealed to the day of redemption, and inherit the promises, as heirs of everlasting salvation.[37]

When an individual is truly saved he is adopted into the family of God. But adoption is based upon the truth of justification. Scripture makes this point when it says: 'But when the fulness of the time came, God sent forth His Son, born of a woman, born under the Law, in order that He might redeem those who were under the Law, that we might receive the adoption as sons' (Gal. 4:4–5). Our adoption as sons can only become a reality if Christ redeems us from the law by bearing its curse for us. Our entire relationship with God, then, is grounded upon a legal declaration sealed in blood—the blood of the Lamb of God who gave himself as a propitiatory sacrifice for sin to satisfy the just claims of the law of God. The believer moves out of the courtroom of God the Judge into the home of God the Father only because Another, our Lord Jesus Christ, stood in his place to bear the consequences of a transgressed law.

Because justification is completely dependent on the work of Christ, it is perfect and eternal in nature. Christ imparts *eternal* life (Jn. 3:16), and his work accomplishes an *eternal* redemption (Heb. 9:12) and provides an *eternal* inheritance (Heb. 9:15; 1 Pet. 1:4). Once a man is justified, therefore, he cannot lose that grace. The scriptures speak with certainty about the assurance of eternal salvation. Jesus himself makes the following statements:

> Truly, truly, I say to you, he who hears My word , and believes Him who sent Me, has eternal life, and does not come into judgment, but has passed out of death into life (Jn. 5:24).
>
> My sheep hear My voice, and I know them, and they follow Me; and I give eternal life to them, and they shall never perish; and no one shall snatch them out of My hand. My Father who has given them to Me, is greater than all; and no one is able to snatch them out of the Father's hand (Jn. 10:27–29).

Justification is a *state* of forgiveness and acceptance with God which is as perfect and eternal as Christ's own standing. It cannot be improved upon and it cannot be lost:

> Who will bring a charge against God's elect? God is the one who justifies; who is the one who condemns? Christ Jesus is He who died, yes, rather who was raised, who is at the right hand of God, who also intercedes for us. Who shall separate us from the love of Christ? Shall tribulation, or distress, or persecution or famine, or nakedness, or peril, or sword?...But in all these things we overwhelmingly conquer through Him who loved us. For I am convinced that neither death, nor life, nor angels, nor principalities, nor things present, nor things to come, nor powers, nor height, nor depth, nor any other created thing, shall be able to separate us from the love of God, which is in Christ Jesus our Lord (Rom. 8:33–35, 37–39).

That is the biblical position. What is the Roman Catholic teaching?

~ 6 ~

The Roman Catholic Position On Justification

If any one saith that by faith alone the impious is justified, in such wise as to mean, that nothing else is required to cooperate in order to obtaing the grace of justification...let him be anathema (The Council of Trent, Canon IX On Justification)

Roman Catholic theology does not embrace the interpretation of justification as that presented by scripture and the Protestant Reformers. The Roman Church *does* teach that we are justified by grace through faith on account of Christ. What is missing, however, is the word *alone*. By omitting this word the Roman Church redefines grace, faith and justification in a way that undermines and invalidates the teaching of scripture. This will become clear as we examine the specific definitions given these terms by the official Magisterium of the Church of Rome.

The Roman View of the Work of Christ

Rome says that Christ made an atonement for sin, meriting the grace by which a person is justified *but* that the work of Christ is not the *exclusive* cause of an individual's justification and salvation. Ludwig Ott makes this statement:

Christ's redemptive activity finds its apogee in the death of sacrifice on the cross. On this account it is by excellence *but not exclusively* the efficient cause of our redemption....No one can be just to whom the merits of Christ's passion have not been communicated. It is a fundamental doctrine of St. Paul that salvation can be acquired only by the grace merited by Christ.[38]

According to the Church of Rome, Christ did not accomplish a full, finished and completed salvation in his work of atonement. His death on the cross merited grace which is then channeled to the individual through the Roman Catholic Church and its sacraments. Grace is not the activity of God in Christ purchasing and accomplishing salvation and eternal life and applying this to man as a gift. And it is not a completed work. Rather, grace is a supernatural quality, infused into the soul of man through the sacraments, enabling him to do works of expiation and righteousness. These works then become the basis of justification. In the Roman theology of justification there is an ongoing need to deal with sin in order to maintain a state of grace, and a need for positive acts of righteousness, which originate from that grace and then become the basis for one's justification. So man's works must be added to the work of Christ, in particular, the work of the sacraments. Consequently, justification is not a once–for–all declaration of righteousness based upon the imputed righteousness of Christ, but a process that is dependent upon the righteousness of man produced through infused grace.

The Sacraments

In Roman Catholic teaching there is no salvation apart from participation in the sacraments mediated through its priesthood. The Roman Church teaches that *she* is the mediator between Christ and the individual. Saving grace is mediated through these sacraments. John Hardon, author of *The Question and Answer Catholic Catechism* (which carries the official authorization of the Vatican) says this:

Why did Christ establish the Church?

Christ established the Church as the universal sacrament of salvation.

How is the Church the universal sacrament of salvation?

The Church is the universal sacrament of salvation as the divinely instituted means of conferring grace on all the members of the human family.

What does the Catholic Church believe about the forgiveness of sins?

She believes it is God's will that no one is forgiven except through the merits of Jesus Christ and that these merits are uniquely channeled through the Church He founded. Consequently, even as the Church is the universal sacrament of salvation, she is also the universal sacrament of reconciliation.

How does the Church communicate the merits of Christ's mercy to sinners?

The Church communicates the merits of Christ's mercy to sinners through the Mass and the sacraments and all the prayers and good works of the faithful.

Are the sacraments necessary for salvation?

According to the way God has willed that we be saved the sacraments are necessary for salvation.[39]

These words clearly express the official position of the Church of Rome. There is no salvation apart from participation in the sacraments of the Roman Catholic Church. There is no other means of obtaining saving grace. Hardon's words echo the teaching of the Council of Trent:

If any one saith that the sacraments of the New Law are not necessary unto salvation...and that without them, or without the desire thereof, men obtain from God, through faith alone, the grace of justification...let him be anathema.[40]

According to Rome, there are three main sacraments necessary for justification and ultimate salvation. These sacraments communicate grace to an individual and help to maintain him in a state of sanctifying grace. They are baptism, penance, and the eucharist/mass. Through baptism, an individual is brought into a state of regeneration and sanctifying grace. The guilt and punishment for original sin and for all sins committed up to the point of baptism is forgiven in the sacrament of baptism. However, sins committed after baptism must be dealt with through the sacraments of penance and the mass. This is especially true for mortal sin which is said to kill the spiritual life in the soul and cause the loss of sanctifying grace and, therefore, of justification. In order to regain the state of grace the individual must participate in the sacraments. As Ott stated, the atonement of Christ is not the exclusive cause of man's redemption. Man must supplement the work of Christ for sins committed after baptism by partially atoning and expiating his own sin through penance. Trent states that no one can be justified apart from the sacrament of penance (the confession of sin to a priest, receiving his absolution and performing the required penance):

> As regards those who, by sin, have fallen from the received grace of Justification, they may again be justified...through the sacrament of Penance...For, on behalf of those who fall into sins after baptism, Christ Jesus instituted the sacrament of Penance...and therein are included not only a cessation from sins, and a detestation thereof, or, a contrite and humble heart, but also the sacramental confession of said sins...and sacerdotal absolution; and likewise satisfaction by fasts, alms, prayers, and the other pious exercises of the spiritual life...for the temporal punishment, which...is not always wholly remitted.
>
> If any one saith that he who has fallen after baptism...is able to recover the justice which he ha s lost...by faith alone

without the sacrament of Penance...let him be anathema.[41]

John Hardon also emphasizes the necessity of penance as a work of expiation:

> Penance is...necessary because we must expiate and make reparation for the punishment which is due our sins...We make satisfaction for our sins by every good act we perform in the state of grace but especially by prayer, penance and the practice of charity.[42]

In addition to Penance the Church teaches the necessity for the mass as an expiation for sins committed after baptism. The mass is the re–sacrifice of Jesus Christ as a propitiation for sin. It is declared by Trent to be a propitiatory sacrifice and necessary for salvation:

> In this divine sacrifice...that same Christ is contained and immolated in an unbloody manner who once offered himself in a bloody manner on the altar of the cross...This sacrifice is truly propitiatory...If any one saith, that the sacrifice of the mass is only a sacrifice of praise and thanksgiving; or that it is a bare commemoration of the sacrifice consummated on the cross, but not a propitiatory sacrifice...and that it ought not to be offered for the living and dead for sins, pains, satisfactions and other necessities: let him be anathema.[43]

John Hardon says:

> The Sacrifice of the altar... is no mere empty commemoration of the Passion and death of Jesus Christ, but a true and proper act of sacrifice. Christ, the eternal High Priest, in an unbloody way offers himself a most acceptable Victim to the eternal Father *as He did upon the Cross*...In the Mass, no less than on Calvary, Jesus really offers His life to His heavenly Father...The Mass, therefore, no less than the Cross, is expiatory for sins (emphasis mine).[44]

Note the assertion here that in the mass Christ offers himself as a Victim for sin in sacrifice just as he did on Calvary. The mass, no less than Calvary, is expiatory for sin because the mass is supposedly the same sacrifice as Calvary. According to Rome, then, the offering of Christ in sacrifice is not finished but continues and is perpetuated through time. But such teaching contradicts scripture. The word of God teaches that Christ has made a complete propitiation for sin through his once–for–all sacrifice of atonement. It is finished. Scripture teaches that Christ's sacrifice, the offering of his body and his death were once–for–all and *cannot be repeated*. Since Christ cannot die again there is no more sacrifice for sin and therefore the mass *cannot* be the same sacrifice as Calvary. To suggest that a sacrament is necessary to continue to offer Christ's body and blood to make sacrifice for sin is completely antithetical to the teaching of scripture and undermines the sufficiency of Christ's work.

This teaching of the mass as a perpetuation of the sacrifice of Christ which is propitaitory for sin was a point of universal opposition by the Reformers. They vigorously objected to this teaching on scriptural grounds that it made void the cross of Christ. These comments from Scottish Reformer, John Knox, and English Reformer, Nicholas Ridley are representative:

John Knox: How can you deny the opinion of your Mass to be false and vain? You say it is a sacrifice for sin, but Jesus Christ and Paul say, The only death of Christ was sufficient for sin, and after it resteth none other sacrifice...I know you will say, it is none other sacrifice, but the self same, save that it is iterated (repeated) and renewed. But the words of Paul bind you more straitly than that so you may escape: for in his whole disputation, contendeth he not only that there is no other sacrifice for sin, but also that the self same sacrifice, once offered, is sufficient, and never may be offered again. For otherwise of no greater price, value, nor extenuation, should the death of Christ be, than the death of those beasts which were offered under the Law: which are proved to be of none effect, nor strength, because it behooves them often times to be repeated. The Apostle, by comparing Jesus Christ to the Levitical priests, and his sacrifice unto theirs, maketh the matter plain that Christ might be offered but once.[45]

Nicholas Ridley: Concerning the Romish mass which is used at this day or the lively sacrifice thereof, propitiatory and available for the sins of the quick and the dead, the holy Scripture hath not so much as one syllable...Now the falseness of the proposition, after the meaning of the schoolmen and the Roman Church and impiety in that sense which the words seem to import is this, that they, leaning to the foundation of their fond transubstantiation, would make the quick and lively body of Christ's flesh, united and knit to the divinity, to lurk under the accidents and outward shows of bread and wine; which is very false...And they, building upon this foundation, do hold that the same body is offered unto God by the priest in his daily massings to put away the sins of the quick and the dead. Whereas by the Apostle to the Hebrews it is evident that there is but one oblation and one true and lively sacrifice of the church offered upon the altar of the cross, which was, is and ever shall be for ever the propitiation for the sins of the whole world, and where there is remission of the same there is (saith the Apostle) no more offering for sin.[46]

In addition to expiation through personal penance and the mass, the Roman Catholic Church also teaches that sin can be expiated through the sufferings of purgatory after one dies and through indulgences. Many are acquainted with the fact that the doctrines of purgatory and indulgences were the catalyst for the Reformation but are unaware that they are still part of the official teaching of the Church. While the abuses of the doctrine of indulgences which led to the Reformation have been repudiated, the actual doctrine itself is still in force. The Church of Rome teaches that through indulgences the temporal punishment for sin can be expiated.

Indulgences are applied through the authority of the pope from what is known as the Treasury of Satisfaction or Merit. This treasury consists of the merit of Christ in addition to the merit of all the saints and can be applied to individuals as remission for sins thereby mitigating the punishment due them either here or in purgatory.

Through its doctrines of confession and penance, the mass, purgatory and indulgences the Church of Rome adds sacramental and moral works to the work of Christ. Justification and salvation are not through Christ *alone* but are instead a cooperative effort between Christ *and* man. Rome claims that it teaches justification by grace alone through the merits of Christ alone. The problem is that her interpretation is not the *scriptural* teaching of grace alone and Christ alone. Just using the word does not mean that one is using it in a scriptural way. After all, Pelagius did not deny the need for grace. He used the term and affirmed it. The problem was not in the use of the word but in the interpretation he applied to it. Though he used the word his interpretation undermined its biblical meaning. This is precisely what the Roman Catholic Church has done with respect to its interpretation of grace and the work of Christ. While affirming these biblical doctrines, its interpretation of what they mean actually undermines their biblical meaning. When scripture says that justification is by grace on account of Christ it means on account of Christ *exclusively*, completely apart from the works of man or sacraments.

The Roman Teaching of Grace and Justification

When Rome states that an individual is justified by grace she means that grace has been infused into the soul of man. This *makes* him righteous before God and enables him to perform acts of righteousness. These then become the basis of justification and the means whereby he merits heaven. Justification is a process then by which the individual is *made righteous* in a moral sense. The Roman Catholic Church interprets the phrase *the righteousness of God* to mean a righteousness which has its source in the grace of God, channeled through sacraments. But the righteousness itself is the work of man cooperating with that grace. The righteousness of God then is *not* the righteousness of Christ but rather the righteousness of man which results from the gift of grace, the source of which is God. The Roman Catholic theologian William Marshner explains the Roman Catholic position in these words:

> Now, if what Paul means by *dikaiosune theou* (righteousness of God) is not something to remain in God but something to be conferred on us, then we must reckon with that mysterious possibility: a quality of man which is the property of God! Does St. Paul say anything to indicate a knowledge of this possibility? Indeed he does: 'God has made him who knew no sin to be sin for us, so that we in him might become justice of God' (II Cor. 5:21)...It is not a question of replacement but of *participation*, and the participation is real in both directions. First in Jesus: just as really as the Word took our humanity, just that really his humanity became God. And then in us: just as really as Christ–God took our sins (so really that even the Father forsook Him—Mark 15:34), just that really we receive God's justice. For if we dare to believe that in the Incarnation our nature, without ceasing to be a human nature, received *God's* subsistence, then we may easily believe that we, in Christ, receive *God's* justice as our quality. In fact, St. Paul even has a name for this quality. In the very next verse (II Cor. 6:1) he says: 'As God's co–workers, we beg you once again not to have received God's grace in vain.' What we should not 'receive in vain' is exactly what Paul has just said we have 'become' in Christ. God's justice *is* His grace, a gift *given* to men. That is why the justice *of God* is identically 'the justice which *comes from* God through faith' (Philippians 3:9). What emerges from these texts then, is the *existence* in man of a justice conferred by God.[47]

Marshner equates the righteousness of God in justification with the righteousness of man in sanctification. This view is a fundamental contradiction of the biblical teaching that the righteousness of God in justification is the righteousness of Christ in his work of atonement. Marshner is correct in stating that just as our sins were imputed to Christ, so a real righteousness is given to the believer. However, it is a righteousness that is already complete and not something that must be worked out by man. We can agree with him when he says that 'God's justice *is* His grace, a gift given to men.' This is the point the Reformers made in their controversy with Rome. God's grace in justification is the provision of a completed, finished righteousness given as a gift which eternally justifies us in the eyes of God. But Marshner misinterprets the scriptures when he refers to this righteousness as the process of sanctification in the life of the believer, rather than the righteousness of Christ himself. By defining justifying grace as God's gift of the righteousness of sanctification, Marshner, and Roman Catholicism as a whole, misinterprets the biblical meaning of grace with respect to justification.

The Council of Trent explicitly condemned the biblical teaching of the imputed righteousness of Christ himself for justification:

If any one saith, that men are just without *the justice of Christ*, whereby he merited for us to be justified; or that it is *by that justice itself* that they are *formally just*, let him be anathema.[48]

Trent teaches that men are justified by the righteousness of Christ *only* in the sense that in his atonement he has merited the grace which is infused into man for salvation. Trent denied that men are justified by the righteousness of Christ *alone* imputed to the believer. Trent taught that the righteousness which justifies is the work of the regenerated believer cooperating with the grace that Christ merited. So justification is equated with regeneration and sanctification.

Rome does not acknowledge sanctification and justification as separate works of God in salvation. It makes human works the basis for justification which merit eternal life:

> Justification...is not the remission of sins merely, but also the sanctification and renewal of the inward man.
>
> If any one saith, that the good works of the one that is justified are in such manner the gifts of God, that they are not also the good merits of him that is justified, by the good works which he performs through the grace of God and the merit of Jesus Christ, whose living member he is, and does not truly merit increase in grace, eternal life, and the attainment of eternal life, if so be, that he depart in grace, and an increase in glory, let him be anathema.[49]

Ludwig Ott emphasizes this in these words:

> Justification is the declaration of the righteousness of the believer before the judgment seat of Christ...The Council of Trent teaches that for the justified eternal life is both a gift or grace promised by God and a reward for his own good works and merits... According to Holy Writ, eternal blessedness in heaven is the reward...for good works performed on this earth, and rewards and merit are correlative concepts.[50]

John Hardon likewise confirms this point of view when he writes:

> Habitual or sanctifying grace is a supernatural quality that dwells in the human soul, by which a person shares in the divine nature, becomes a temple of the Holy Spirit, a friend of God, his adopted child, and *able to perform actions meriting eternal life* (emphasis mine).[51]

So Roman Catholic theology teaches that justification is obtained by receiving grace through baptism, and is maintained through the sacrament of penance, the mass and the works of sanctification which in turn merit eternal life. It is important to point out that sanctification in Roman Catholic theology is not only the righteous acts of individuals cooperating with the grace of God but participation in the sacraments of the Church. A state of sanctifying grace, by which a person is justified, cannot be maintained apart from the sacraments. Justification then is *not* by grace alone (in the biblical sense) or on account of Christ alone (in the biblical sense). Therefore it is not by faith alone (in the biblical sense). In fact, the Council of Trent condemned the teaching of justification by faith alone stating:

> If anyone saith that by faith alone the impious is justified in such wise as to mean that nothing else is required to cooperate in order to obtaining the grace of Justification...let him be anathema...After this Catholic doctrine on justification which whosoever does not faithfully and firmly accept cannot be justified...[52]

John Gerstner gives a clear and concise summation of the Roman Catholic view of justification in contrast to the Protestant view in these words:

> Some Romanists will say that they too teach justification by grace—by Christ's righteousness, in fact. But the righteous-ness of Christ which they claim justifies is not Christ's own personal righteousness reckoned or credited or given or imputed to believers. Romanists refer to the righteousness which Christ works into the life of the believer or infuses into him in his own living and behavior. It is not Christ's personal righteousness but the believer's personal righteousness, which he performs by the grace of God. It is Christ's righteousness versus the believer's own righteousness. It is Christ's achievement versus the Christian's achievement. It is an imputed righteousness not an infused righteousness. It is a gift of God versus an accomplishment of man. These two righteousnesses are as different as righteousnesses could

conceivably be. It does come down to the way it has been popularly stated for the last four and a half centuries: Protestantism's salvation by faith versus Rome's salvation by works...The Protestant trusts Christ to save him and the Catholic trusts Christ to help him save himself. It is faith versus works. Or, as the Spirit of God puts it in Romans 4:16 (NIV), 'Therefore, the promise comes by faith, so that it may be by grace, and may be guaranteed to all Abraham's offspring.' It is 'by faith *so that it may be by* grace...' If a Romanist wants to be saved by grace alone, it will have to be by faith alone. 'The promise comes by faith so that it may be by grace.' You can't be saved 'sola gratia' except 'sola fide.'...We agree with Roman friends—salvation *is* by grace. That is the reason it must be by faith. If it is a salvation based on works that come from grace, it is not based on grace but on the Christian's works that come from grace. The works that come from grace must *prove* grace but they cannot *be* grace. They may come from, be derivative of, a consequence of, but they cannot be identified with it. Faith is merely union with Christ who is our righteousness, our grace, our salvation. 1 Corinthians 1:30, 'It is because of Him that you are in Christ Jesus who has become for us wisdom from God,' that is, our righteousness, holiness, and redemption. Christ is our righteousness. Our righteousness does not *result* from His righteousness, it is His righteousness.[53]

Faith

Roman Catholicism teaches that saving faith is not trust in Christ *alone* for justification and salvation. While the Church of Rome affirms the necessity for faith in the justification of adults, her definition is different from that of the scriptures and the teaching of the Protestant Church. To a Roman Catholic, justifying faith is called *dogmatic* faith. This has to do with the doctrinal content of the faith necessary to be believed for salvation. Essentially it means intellectual assent to eveything the Church teaches. In order to be saved an individual must believe and hold to every doctrine dogmatically defined by the Roman Catholic Church. This entails not only the teaching of the Creed, the sacraments and justification but also the doctrines related to the Papacy (papal rule and infallibility), Mary (immaculate conception and assumption), the canon of scripture and purgatory. Vatican I states that it is necessary for salvation that an individual believe not only all that is revealed in scripture but also everything defined and proposed by the Church. To reject anything officially taught by the Roman Church is to reject saving faith and to forfeit both justification and eternal life:

> Further, all those things are to be believed with divine and Catholic faith which are contained in the Word of God, written or handed down, and which the Church, either by a solemn judgment, or by her ordinary and universal magisterium, proposes for belief as having been divinely revealed. And since, without faith, it is impossible to please God, and to attain to the fellowship of his children, therefore without faith no one has ever attained justification, nor will any one obtain eternal life unless he shall have persevered in faith unto the end.[54]

Ludwig Ott explains the relationship of Dogmas defined by the Church and faith in these words:

> By dogma in the strict sense is understood a truth immediately (formally) revealed by God which has been proposed by the Teaching Authority of the Church to be believed as such. Two factors or elements may be distinguished in the concept of dogma:
> A) An immediate Divine Revelation of the particular Dogma...i.e., the Dogma must be immediately revealed by God either explicitly (explicite) or inclusively (implicite), and therefore be contained in the sources of Revelation (Holy Writ or Tradition).

B) The Promulgation of the Dogma by the Teaching Authority of the Church (propositio Ecclesiae). *This implies, not merely the promulgation of the Truth, but also the obligation on the part of the Faithful of believing the Truth.* This promulgation by the Church may be either in an extraordinary manner through a solemn decision of faith made by the Pope or a General Council (Iudicium solemns) or through the ordinary and general teaching power of the Church (Magisterium ordinarium et universale). The latter may be found easily in the catechisms issued by the Bishops.

Dogma in its strict signification is the object of both Divine Faith (Fides Divina) and Catholic Faith (Fides Catholica); it is the object of the Divine Faith...by reason of its Divine Revelation; it is the object of Catholic Faith...on account of its infallible doctrinal definition by the Church. If a baptised person deliberately denies or doubts a dogma properly so-called, he is guilty of the sin of heresy (Codex Iuris Canonici 1325, Par. 2), and automatically becomes subject to the punishment of excommunication *(Codex Iuris Canonici* 2314, Par. I).

As far as the content of justifying faith is concerned, the so-called fiducial faith does not suffice. What is demanded is theological or dogmatic faith (confessional faith) which consists in the firm acceptance of the Divine truths of Revelation, on the authority of God Revealing...*According to the testimony of Holy Writ, faith and indeed dogmatic faith, is the indispensable prerequisite for the achieving of eternal salvation* (emphasis added).[55]

And John Hardon says:

What must a Catholic believe with divine faith?

A Catholic must believe with divine faith the whole of revelation, which is contained in the written word of God and in Sacred Tradition.

Can a person be a Catholic if he believes most, but not all, the teachings of revelation?

A person cannot be a Catholic if he rejects even a single teaching that he knows has been revealed by God.

What will happen to those who lack 'the faith necessary for salvation'?

Those will not be saved who lack the necessary faith because of their own sinful neglect or conduct. As Christ declared, 'He who does not believe will be condemned' (Mark 16:16).

Why is divine faith called catholic?

Divine faith is called catholic or universal because a believer must accept everything God has revealed. He may not be selective about what he chooses to believe.[56]

The dogmatic teachings of Vatican I are a perfect example of this point of view. After giving extensive teaching on the need to be submitted to the bishop of Rome for salvation the Council makes this statement: *This is the teaching of Catholic truth from which no one can deviate without loss of faith and salvation.*[57] There are similar statements made by the Bishops of Rome in their decrees on Mary, as well as numerous anathemas which have accompanied the doctrinal promulgations of Trent and Vatican I on the sacraments and the papacy on papal rule and infallibility. According to Rome, all these dogmas *must* be believed and embraced for salvation. But where are these teachings found in scripture? Where are we told that it is necessary to believe in the assumption of Mary or papal infallibility in order to experience salvation? Such teachings not only are absent from scripture, but from the teaching of the Church historically. Not one of these doctrines was taught in the early Church.

From a Roman Catholic perspective, the concept of saving faith is far removed from the biblical teaching of commitment to and simple trust in Christ *alone* for salvation. The Roman Catholic Church has distorted th e gospel of grace. It has fallen into the same Galatian error of legalism (a sacerdotal/ sacramental/works salvation) addressed by Paul in his letter to the Galatian Churches. In that letter Paul dealt with the heresy of the Judaizers, who attempted to add the Jewish ceremonial law to faith in Christ as a basis for salvation. Temple worship and the ceremonial law included circumcision, an altar, daily sacrifices, a laver of water, priests, a high priest, special priestly and high priestly vestments and robes, candles, incense and shewbread. In the routine religious life of the average Jew there were feast days, prayers, fasts, adherence to the tradition of the elders and certain dietary restrictions. All of these things were included in the Judaizers' teaching on salvation. So it was Jesus *plus* the Jewish system. How does this relate to Roman Catholicism? The doctrines of salvation embraced by Rome are, in principle, identical to the Judaizers. The Roman Church teaches that salvation is achieved by believing that Jesus is the Son of God who died for sin, by being baptized, by being a part of the Roman Catholic Church, by striving to keep the Ten Commandments and partaking of the sacramental system (which involves ongoing sacrifices, altars, priests, a high priest, along with the exercises of prayers, fasts, almsgiving, penances and until recently adherence to certain dietary regulations). The following lists demonstrate the parallels between Roman Catholicism and the Judaizers:

JUDAIZERS	ROMAN CATHOLICISM
1. Belief in Jesus as Messiah and Son of God	1. Belief in Jesus as Messiah and Son of God
2. Circumcision	2. Baptism
3. Become a Jew	3. Become a Roman Catholic
4. Sacrificial System	4. Sacrificial System
5. Priests	5. Priests
6. High Priests	6. High Priests
7. Altars	7. Altars
8. Feast Days	8. Feast Days

9. Laver of Water	9. Font of Holy Water
10. Dietary Regulations	10. Dietary Regulations (Until Recently)
11. Candles	11. Candles
12. Incense	12. Incense
13. Shew Bread	13. Shew Bread
14. Keep the Ten Commandments	14. Keep the Ten Commandments
15. Traditions of the Elders	15. Traditions of the Fathers

The parallels are obvious. The Roman Catholic teaching on salvation is essentially the same as that preached by the Judaizers. Paul warned the Galatian believers that if they embraced this false gospel they would actually desert Christ (Gal. 1:6). Those evangelicals who would promote spiritual cohabitation with the Church of Rome need to heed to the warning of Paul. He saw no basis for unity with the Judaizers even though they professed faith in Christ. Likewise, there is no basis for unity with the Church of Rome today. If evangelicals jettison the Reformation gospel distinctives for so called unity with Rome they will deny Christ.

~ 7 ~

Sanctification

Pursue....sanctification without which no one will see the Lord (Heb. 12:14)

Like justification, sanctification is an essential part of the overall work of salvation. It must be noted again that scripture teaches that sanctification cannot be separated from justification. *There is no salvation without sanctification.* No one can be justified who is not at the same time being sanctified for the God who justifies also sanctifies. Hebrews 2:11 states: 'For both He who sanctifies and those who are sanctified are all from one Father, for which reason He is not ashamed to call them brethren.' Christ himself says: 'Not everyone who says to Me, "Lord, Lord," will enter the kingdom of heaven; but *he who does the will of My Father* who is in heaven' (Mt. 7:21). The apostle John warns us that a profession of salvation will be proved by a life of obedience to the commandments of God, *i.e.* a life of sanctification (1 Jn. 2:3–6). Paul teaches that only those who have forsaken sin and are walking in holiness of life will inherit the kingdom of God (1 Cor. 6:9–11; Eph. 5:5–6; Gal. 5:19–21). James says that a profession of faith without any accompanying works of sanctification is a dead faith and therefore non–saving (Js. 2:14–21). The theology of the Reformation was unanimous in declaring this truth. Note, for example, the following comments by John Calvin:

Why, then, are we justified by faith? Because by faith we

101

grasp Christ's righteousness, by which alone we are reconciled to God. Yet you could not grasp this without at the same time grasping sanctification also. For he 'is given unto us for righteousness, wisdom, sanctification, and redemption' (1 Cor 1:30). Therefore Christ justifies no one whom he does not at the same time sanctify. These benefits are joined together by an everlasting and indissoluble bond, so that those whom he illumines by his wisdom, he redeems; those whom he redeems, he justifies; those whom he justifies, he sanctifies. But, since the question concerns only righteousness and sanctification, let us dwell upon these. Although we may distinguish them, Christ contains both of them inseparably in himself. Do you wish, then, to attain righteousness in Christ? You must first possess Christ; but you cannot possess him without being made partaker of his sanctification, because he cannot be divided into pieces (1 Cor. 1:13). Since, therefore, it is solely by expending himself that the Lord gives us these benefits to enjoy, he bestows both of them at the same time, the one never without the other. Thus it is clear how true it is that we are justified not without works yet not through works, since in our sharing in Christ, which justifies us, sanctification is just as much included as righteousness.[58]

We saw in an earlier chapter the affirmation of works by Philip Melanchthon and Thomas Cranmer. Martin Luther likewise emphasized the necessity for the works of sanctification in salvation:

From all this it is easy to perceive on what principle good works are to be cast aside or embraced, and by what rule all teachings put forth concerning works are to be understood. For if works are brought forward as grounds of justification, and are done under the false persuasion that we can pretend to be justified by them, they lay on us the yoke of necessity, and extinguish liberty along with faith, and by this very addition to their use they become no longer good, but really worthy of condemnation. For such works are not free, but blaspheme the grace of God, to which alone it belongs to justify and save through faith. Works cannot accomplish this, and yet, with impious presumption, through our folly, they take on themselves to do so; and thus break in with violence upon the office and glory of grace.

We do not then reject good works; nay, we embrace them and teach them in the highest degree. It is not on their own account that we condemn them, but on account of this impious addition to them and the preverse notion of seeking justification from them. It is not from works that we are set free by the faith of Christ, but from belief in works, that is from foolishly presuming to seek justification through works. Faith redeems our consciences, makes them upright, and preserves them, since by it we recognise the truth that justification does not depend on our works, although good works neither can nor ought to be absent...[59]

The following comments from the Scottish *Confession of Faith* from the mid sixteenth century represents the views of John Knox and the Protestant Church on the necessity for sanctification:

So that the cause of Good works we confess to be, not our free will, but the Spirit of the Lord Jesus who, dwelling in our hearts by true faith, brings forth such good works as God hath prepared for us to walk into: for this we most boldly affirm, that blasphemy it is to say that Christ Jesus abides in the hearts of such as in whom there is no spirit of Sanctification. And therefore we fear not to affirm that murderers, oppressors, cruel persecuters, adulterers, whoremongers, filthy persons, idolators, drunkards, thieves, and all workers of iniquity, have neither true faith, neither any portion of the spirit of Sanctification, which proceedeth from the Lord Jesus so long as they obstinately continue in their wickedness. For how soon that ever the spirit of the Lord Jesus (which God's elect children receive by true faith), takes possession in the heart of any man, so soon does He regenerate and renew the same man; so that he begins to hate that which before he loved, and begins to love that which before he hated...But the Spirit of God, which giveth witnessing to our spirit, that we are the sons of God, makes us to resist the devil, to abhor filthy pleasures, to groan in God's presence for deliverance from this bondage of corruption; and finally, so to triumph over sin that it reign not in our mortal bodies...The sons of God...do fight against sin, do sob and mourn, when they perceive themselves tempted to iniquity; and if they fall, they rise again with earnest and unfeigned repentance. And these things they do not by their own power, but the power of the Lord Jesus (without whom they are able to do nothing) worketh in them all that is good.[60]

The Westminster Confession is very clear in stating that saving faith means a receiving of and trusting in Christ for justification and sanctification:

The principal acts of saving faith are, accepting, receiving, and resting upon Christ alone for justification, sanctification and eternal life, by virtue of the covenant of grace.[61]

A.A. Hodge sums up the Reformed teaching with this warning:

Now, every Christian who really has experienced the grace of Christ must, unless very greatly prejudiced, recognize the fact that this work of sanctification is the *end* and the *crown* of the whole process of salvation. We insist upon and put forward distinctly the great doctrine of justification as a means to an end. It is absolutely necessary as the condition of that faith which is the necessary source of regeneration and sanctification; and every person who is a Christian must recognize the fact that not only will it issue in sanctification, but it must begin in sanctification. This element must be recognized as characteristic of the Christian experience from the first to the last. And any man who thinks that he is a Christian, and that he has accepted Christ for justification when he did not at the same time accept Christ for sanctification, is miserably deluded in that very experience. He is in danger of falling under the judgment of which Paul admonishes when he speaks of the wrath of God coming down from heaven upon all ungodliness and unrighteousness of men, and with special reference to those who 'hold the truth in unrighteousness.'[62]

Sanctification and justification are inseparably linked through union with Christ. When this union takes place the Christian becomes a slave of Christ and, as a result, a slave of righteousness (Rom. 6:1–22). Consequently, saving faith that unites a person to Christ will always manifest the reality of that union in progressive sanctification. Scripture refers to this as works or fruit.

But sanctification has two aspects. There is a *positional* sanctification which is followed by a *progressive* sanctification. Just as there are two aspects to the nature of sin (the disposition of the heart and consequential behavior), so there are two parts to sanctification. Sanctification relates first to God as a person (positional) and secondarily to his will (progressive). It deals with the disposition of the heart being wholly set apart to God and then with behavioral obedience which flows out of the relationship. In other words, for there to be a sanctified life there must first of all be a sanctified heart—a heart set apart and devoted to God. It is what scripture calls a circumcised heart. Martyn Lloyd–Jones distinguishes these two aspects of sanctification:

The main characteristic of people who are sanctified is that God is in the center of their lives. That is the first thing we may say about them. Before we get them to say what they do or do not do with regard to a particular action, we must be clear about the central, primary, most vital thing...Sanctification is that which separates us from sin unto

God...The essence of sanctification is that I love God in whom I believe and who has been revealed to me, with the whole of my being...Sanctification is a matter of being rightly related to God, and becoming entirely devoted to him...not only separated from the world but separated unto God and sharing his life.[63]

In Romans 6:22 Paul gives a description of the Christian and the nature of the salvation that God accomplishes: 'Therefore, having been freed from sin and enslaved to God, you derive your fruit resulting in sanctification and the outcome eternal life.' The sanctified life then, or fruit in the Christian's life, is directly related to his having been set free from sin and enslaved to God. There can be no obedience to the will of God without first being submitted to the person of God. This is obvious from the phrase 'enslaved to God.' The word 'enslaved' is a form of the Greek word *doulos*. It means a bondslave. The corresponding or complementary word is the Greek *kyrios* or Lord. A *doulos* is one who is in relationship with one who is Lord. This means that unless an individual has entered a relationship with God as Lord and become a *doulos* he has never been set free from sin. J.I. Packer states it succinctly: 'Where Christ does not rule, sin does.'[64]

To understand in practical terms the meaning of the word *doulos* it would be helpful to define it in the context of the Greek culture from which it is derived. The word literally means a slave. *The Dictionary of New Testament Theology* gives the following background on the word:

For the Attic (Greek), personal freedom was his prized possession. To be independent of others and to manage his own life and to live as he chooses is of the essence of such freedom. The *doulos* belonged by nature not to himself, but to someone else...Because *douleuo* involved the abrogation of one's own autonomy and the subordination of one's will to that of another, the Greek felt only revulsion and contempt for the position of a slave...*Douleuein* in the sense of dependence and subordination in service is debasing and contemptible...That which the Greeks regarded as the highest form of freedom becomes in the (New Testament) the source of man's most abject bondage. Man, bent upon himself, obstinately waves God's help aside and busies himself in running his own life in his own strength, trusting in his own resources, and falls into the grip of fear...Christ's redemption frees one for obedient service under the command of the *Kyrios*...and leads one into the service of righteousness in the new Spirit-given nature (Rom. 6:18; 7:6).[65]

The idea of personal autonomy and independence is the antithesis of what it means to be a *doulos*. A *doulos* is one who is owned by another. Therefore a true Christian is one who has renunciated personal autonomy and independence from God. He has submitted his life to Christ as Lord to become the possession of Christ. He then begins to *live* in subjection to Christ and his will.

Progressive sanctification begins with a relationship in being set apart unto God as his servant. From that relationship flows a life of progressive sanctification or obedience. Positional sanctification is foundational to progressive sanctification. John Murray emphasizes this in these comments:

When we speak of sanctification we generally think of it as a process by which the believer is gradually transformed in heart, mind, will, and conduct, and conformed more and more to the will of God and to the image of Christ, until at death the disembodied spirit is made perfect in holiness, and at the resurrection his body likewise will be conformed to the likeness of the body of Christ's glory. It is biblical to apply the term 'sanctification' to this process of transformation and conformation. But it is a fact too frequently overlooked that in the New Testament the most characteristic terms that refer to sanctification are used, not of a process, but of a once–for–all definitive act.

We properly think of calling, regeneration, justification, and adoption as acts of God effected once for all, and not requiring or admitting of repetition. It is of their nature to be definitive. But a considerable part of the New Testament teaching places sanctification in this category...We are thus compelled to take account of the fact that the language of sanctification is used with reference to some decisive action that occurs at the inception of the Christian life, and one that characterizes the people of God in their identity as called effectually by God's grace. It would be, therefore, a deflection from biblical patterns of language and conception to think of sanctification exclusively in terms of a progressive work.

What is this sanctification? No passage in the New Testament is more instructive than Romans 6:1–7:6. The teaching here is oriented against the question with which Paul begins: 'Shall we continue in sin that grace may abound?'...What does Paul mean? He is using the language of that phenomenon with which we are all familiar, the event of death. When a person dies he is no longer active in the sphere or realm or relation in reference to which he has died. His connection with that realm has been dissolved; he has no further communications with those who still live in that realm, nor do they have with him.

In accord with this analogy, the person who lives in sin, or to sin, lives and acts in the realm of sin—it is the sphere of his life and activity. And the person who died to sin no longer lives in that sphere. His tie with it has been broken, and he has been translated into another realm...This is the decisive cleavage that the apostle has in view; it is the foundation upon which rests his whole conception of a believer's life, and it is a cleavage, a breach, a translation as really and decisively true in the sphere of moral and religious relationship as in ordinary experience of death. There is a once–for–all definitive and irreversible breach with the realm in which sin reigns in and unto death...This means that there is a decisive and definitive breach with the power and service of sin in the case of every one who has come under the control of the provisions of grace.[66]

A life of obedience—progressive sanctification—can only be lived out by a life that is truly consecrated to God. Sanctification is not just a process. It begins with a commitment of life to God. We must differentiate between definitive and progressive sanctification, emphasizing the one as productive of the other, because *apart from this initial commitment to God, there will be no progressive sanctification in behavior.* We may emphasize the necessity for submission to the will of God in Christian experience but if we do not place equal emphasis on the need for submission of heart to God himself we will only call men to morality and not righteousness. Morality is ethical behavior without a heart submitted to God. Righteousness, on the other hand, is ethical behavior that flows out of a right relationship with God. John Owen makes this point when he says:

All obedience unto Christ proceeds from an express subjection of our souls and consciences unto Him...We may learn hence not to satisfy ourselves, or not to rest, in any acts or duties of obedience, in any good works, how good and useful soever in themselves, or howsoever multiplied by us, unless there be a vital principle of holiness in our hearts. A few honest actions, a few useful duties, do satisfy some persons that they are as holy as they should be, or as they need to be...But God expressly rejecteth not only such duties, but the greatest multitude of them, and their most frequent reiteration, if the heart be not antecedently purified and sanctified, if it be not possessed with the principle of grace and holiness'[67]

And John Flavel says:

Sanctification notes a holy dedication of heart and life to God: Our becoming the temples of the living God, separate from all profane sinful practices, to the Lord's only use and service.[68]

While it is true that positionally a believer is viewed as sanctified before God, this is not the whole story about definitive sanctification. As Murray points out, this aspect of sanctification involves a very real and decisive break with the rule and realm of sin. It is just as real in the experience of the believer as progressive sanctification. It is not just theological, it is also experiential.

There is no salvation without sanctification. A holy life is the evidence of saving faith and justification because it is evidence of union with Christ. The Reformers have often been falsely accused of teaching that justification by faith means that the works of sanctification are not necessary in the overall work of salvation. It has been stated by Roman Catholics that Luther and Calvin taught that one could be justified and saved and go on living in sin. William Marshner believes and teaches this as evidenced by the following comments:

Living faith: our quality but God's instrument; good works: our deeds but God's handiwork; our deeds as men *living* in Christ, not the motions of 'graced' zombies still dead in sin— these are the possibilities overlooked by Luther and Calvin but preached by Paul and defined by Trent.[69]

The quotations cited above from the Reformers and the Reformed theologians who followed them prove conclusively that they never taught that men who were justified in Christ remained dead in sin and continued living in it. The Reformers all taught in the strongest possible terms the absolute necessity for sanctification. What they did *not* do was equate sanctification with justification. It is important to note again that the Reformers affirmed what scripture affirms—an imputed righteousness for justification as well as the righteousness of sanctification received through the grace of God by the indwelling Holy Spirit. John Gerstner offers the following clarification of the Protestant teaching in light of the Roman Catholic misrepresentation :

> Romanists have always tried to hang antinomianism on Protestantism. They seem incapable even of understanding 'justification is by faith alone, but not by the faith that is alone,' though that formula has been present since the Reformation.
>
> If this were a true charge it would be a fatal one. If Protestantism thought that a sinner could be saved without becoming godly, it would be an absolute, damning lie. His name is 'Jesus' for He saves His is people *from* their sins, not *in* them. And He saves His people not only from the guilt of sin but from its dominating power as well. If a believer is not changed, he is not a believer. No one can have Christ as Savior for one moment when He is not Lord as well. We can never say too often: 'Justification is by faith alone, but NOT by a faith that is alone.' Justification is by a WORKING faith.
>
> Why does Rome continue to make that centuries–long misrepresentation of justification by faith alone? Because:
>
> First, she knows that faith without works is dead. Second, she hears Protestantism teach justification by faith alone 'apart' from works. Third, she doesn't listen when Protestantism explains that 'apart from works means 'apart from the *merit* of works,' not 'apart from the presence of works.' Fourth, she hears *some* Protestants, who also misunderstand Protestantism, teaching 'easy–believism.' Fifth, she knows 'easy–believism' is an utterly overwhelming argument against Protestantism (which it would be it were true).
>
> Let me explain, therefore, once again what the Protestant biblical doctrine of justification by faith alone apart from works means. Justification with God is apart from the *merit* of works. That does not mean that justification is apart from the existence of works. Christianity teaches justification

apart from the merit of works. Easy–believism teaches justification apart from the existence of works. Faith without the existence of works is dead...Faith with the merit of works is legalism.[70]

Here, an objection is raised by some from within Protestantism regarding this teaching on sanctification: If sanctification is a necessary part of salvation, is that not the same thing as saying that works are necessary for salvation? Are you not collapsing sanctification into justification, making works the basis for justification? The answer is no. Justification is a work of Christ accomplished completely outside of man, given as a gift, applied by God and received by faith when the individual is united to Christ. The righteousness of Christ is imputed to him. But while justification is a legal declaration of righteousness there is more to salvation. Again, justification is but one part of the overall work of salvation. When a man is united to Christ and justified, he is also regenerated and sanctified and begins to manifest this wonderful change in a life of obedience. This comes, as does justification, from union with Christ. It is a separate and distinct work of God in salvation. Justification is a completed, eternal work in its own right. All the work necessary to merit justification and eternal life was accomplished by Christ in man's stead. Therefore the basis for justification is the work of Christ alone. Sanctification is *not* the basis of justification. But sanctification is produced from the same union that justifies. The works of sanctification are the *evidence* of the reality of union with Christ and regeneration and therefore of justification. If a man is not regenerated and sanctified he has never been justified because he is not united to Christ. Martyn Lloyd–Jones expresses it this way:

> Justification is only one step, an initial step, in a process. And the process includes not only justification but regeneration and sanctification and ultimate glorification. Justification

and forgiveness of sins are not ends in and of themselves; they are only steps on a way that leads to final perfection...Some Christians persist in isolating these things, but they are not isolated in the Scriptures...We cannot divorce justification and forgiveness from other parts of truth...God does not justify a man and leave him there. Not at all! If God justifies a man, God has brought that man into the process...And unless we are giving evidence of being in the process and of being perfected by it, there is but one conclusion to draw—we have never been in the kingdom at all, we must go back to the very beginning, we must repent and believe on the Lord Jesus Christ.[71]

This truth needs to be heralded in our day: God justifies no one whom he does not also regenerate and sanctify. God does not justify men through the death of his Son, only to have them continue to live habitually in sin. He does not leave man dead in sin, but supernaturally transforms their very natures through the miracle of the new birth.

~ 8 ~

Regeneration

Truly, truly, I say to you, unless one is born again, he cannot see the kingdom of God (John 3:3)

Regeneration is the exclusive work of God by which he imparts new life to an individual. There is no sanctification or justification apart from regeneration. It is what scripture calls the new creation (2 Cor. 5:17) or being born again (Jn. 3:3–6). The imperative nature of the new birth was taught by Jesus in his conversation with Nicodemus when he said, 'Truly, truly I say to you, unless one is born again, he cannot see the kingdom of God' (Jn. 3:5). Jesus taught that it is not enough that we be religious, moral people. We must be born again, born from above, born of God. We must be recreated on the inside in our very natures or we cannot enter the kingdom of God. As D.A. Carson comments:

> Here was Jesus telling Nicodemus, a respected and conscientious member not only of Israel but of the Sanhedrin, that he cannot enter the kingdom unless he is *born again*...The focus here is not on the potential convert's humility, brokenness of faith, but on the need for *transformation*, for new life from another realm, for the intervention of the Spirit of God.[72]

Regeneration is a sovereign work of God whereby he supernaturally intervenes in a life, creates a new heart, gives new life and enables one to come to Christ. Scripture teaches that it is the Lord who must enlighten the heart to understand truth (Eph. 1:17–18); no man can come to Christ unless the Father first draws him (Jn. 6:44); it is the Lord who opens hearts to understand and respond to the gospel (Acts 16:14); and who causes individuals to be born again (Jn. 3:6–8). Salvation is the exclusive work of God from beginning to end. No man can cause himself to be born again. We are shut up to the grace, power and mercy of God alone. And yet our God delights to do this. To be regenerated is to be supernaturally recreated in the image of Jesus Christ. We have defined the term 'image of Christ' to mean a *doulos* or bondslave of God—one whose entire life is devoted to God. In regeneration, man becomes like Jesus Christ, a *doulos* of God.

Regeneration is another part of the overall work of salvation. It is a transformation and renewal of the inner being where love for self is displaced by love for God. The Reformed view of regeneration is summed up by John Murray:

There is a change that God effects in man, radical and reconstructive in its nature, called new birth, new creation, regeneration, renewal—a change that cannot be accounted for by anything that is in lower terms than the interposition of the almighty power of God....It is the Holy Spirit working directly, efficaciously and irresistibly upon man's heart and mind, making the man over again, and creating him anew after the image of Christ in holiness and righteousness of the truth. A revolution, a reconstruction takes place at the center of man's moral and spiritual being: sin and pollution are dethroned in the citadel of man's being, and righteousness takes its place.

In later Reformed theology the term *regeneration* has been chosen to designate the initial act, that act in which God alone is active, while *conversion* is frequently used to designate the logically subsequent phase in which the person is active as a result of th e grace which the person's consciousness is engaged in the exercise of faith and repentance. Regeneration in this restricted sense is logically antecedent to any saving response in the consciousness or understanding of the subject. Regeneration is a change wrought by the Spirit in order that the person may savingly respond to the summons, or demand of the call, embodied in the gospel call.[73]

God does not leave those he saves in sin and bondage. He frees them through so radical a transformation of nature that it is described in scripture as a new creation: 'If any man is in Christ he is a new creature; the old things have passed away; behold new things have come' (2 Cor. 5:17). This is regeneration.

Much of the Reformation teaching on salvation is misrepresented by Roman Catholics who charge that the Reformers taught that men could be justified yet go on living in sin. This is not only a spurious charge with respect to sanctification but also for regeneration. The comments from the following Reformers demonstrate this fact:

John Calvin: To prove the first point—that God justifies not only by pardoning but by regenerating—he (Osiander) asks whether God leaves as they were by nature those whom he justifies, changing none of their vices. This is exceedingly easy to answer; as Christ cannot be torn into parts, so these two which we perceive in him together and conjointly are inseparable—namely, righteousness and sanctification. Whomever, therefore, God receives into grace, on them he at the same time bestows the spirit of adoption [Rom. 8:15], by whose power he remakes them to his own image...The grace of justification is not separated from regeneration, although they are things distinct.[74]

Huldrych Zwingli: When, therefore, Divine Majesty formed the plan of redeeming man, it did not intend that the world should persist and become inveterate in its wickedness. For if this had been the plan, it would have been better never to have sent a redeemer than to have sent one under such conditions that after redemption there should be no change from our former diseased state. It would have been laughable if He to whom everything that is ever to be is seen as present had determined to deliver man at so great a cost, and yet had intended to allow him to immediately after his deliverance to wallow in his old sins. He proclaims, therefore, at the start, that our lives and characters must be changed. For to be a Christian is nothing less than to be a new man and a new creature (II Cor. 5:17).[75]

Philip Melanchthon: Christianity is freedom because those who do not have the Spirit of Christ cannot in any way perform the law; they are rather subject to the curse of the law. Those who have been renewed by the Spirit of Christ now conform voluntarily even without the law to what the law used to command. The law is the will of God; the Holy Spirit is nothing else than the living will of God and its being in action (*agitatio*). Therefore, when we have been regenerated by the Spirit of God, who is the living will of God, we now will spontaneously that very thing which the law used to demand...Those who are in Christ are led by the Spirit to do the law and they really act by the Spirit. They love and fear God, devote themselves to the needs of their neighbor, and desire to do those very things which the law demanded. They would do them even if no law had been given. Their will is nothing else than the Spirit, the living law.[76]

These comments are representative of the overall teaching of the Reformers demonstrating they did, in fact, insist on the necessity for regeneration and holiness of life in the salvation experience. There is no justification apart from regeneration according to scripture and the Reformers. As R.C. Sproul observes:

Technically   the   term   justification   does   refer   to   the declarative judicial act of God and not to the person who receives the benefit of this declarative act and is said to be justified. The declaration changes the status of the believer and not his or her nature. However, as John Gerstner relentlessly points out, it is not a declaration about or directed toward people who are not changed in their constituent nature. God never declares a change in the status of people who are unchanged in nature...The antinomian error (assumes) that God justifies people who are and remain unchanged. All who are justified possess faith. Faith abides as a necessary condition for justification. All who have faith are regenerate. Reformed theology sees regeneration as a necessary condition for faith. All who are regenerated are changed in their natures. It is not change in our nature wrought by regeneration or our faith that flows from it that is the ground of our justification. That remains solely the imputation of the righteousness of Christ. But that righteousness is not imputed to unbelieving or unregenerate persons.[77]

When Nicodemus was confronted with the teaching of Jesus on the necessity of the new birth he said: 'How can these things be' (Jn. 3:9)? But as D.A. Carson points out, a better translation of what Nicodemus actually said would be: 'How can this happen?':

Nicodemus' incredulous question is not *How can this be?* (NIV), but 'How can this happen?' Doubtless he himself had for years taught others the conditions of entrance to the kingdom of God, conditions cast in terms of obedience to God's commands, devotion to God, happy submission to his will; but here he is facing a condition he has never heard expressed, the absolute requirement of birth from above. Even after Jesus' explanation, he is frankly skeptical that such a birth can take place.[78]

While his question is one of incredulity and skepticism, it is a legitimate one. If regeneration is an absolute requirement for entrance into the kingdom of God then *How can this happen?*, is the obvious question to ask. To answer the question, *how,* we must first address the controversy centered around water baptism.

The Meaning and Place of Baptism

There are those who teach that men are regenerated when they are baptized, a belief commonly referred to as baptismal regeneration. There are others who teach that baptism, while necessary as an act of obedience to Christ and as a public testimony to the reality of one's salvation, is not the means of regeneration. It is rather meant to be the outward testimony of an inward work of grace. The controversy centers around John 3:5 that a man must be 'born of water and the Spirit'. Before looking at this passage it would be helpful to look at the overall teaching of the scriptures on baptism to give context to the words of Jesus.

When the Bible refers to baptism, it does not always mean water baptism. Many scriptures also refer to Spirit baptism. In the baptism of the Holy Spirit, a person separated from Christ is united to him becoming one with Christ, their lives joined in an indissoluble union. Paul speaks of this when he says that 'by one Spirit we were all baptized into one body' (1 Cor. 12:13). This is a *spiritual* union effected by a spiritual baptism as part of the overall work of salvation. It has nothing to do with water baptism. Paul makes this point when speaking of the conversion of the Ephesians: 'In Him, you also, after listening to the message of truth, the gospel of your salvation—having also believed, you were sealed in Him with the Holy Spirit of promise' (Eph. 1:13).

Spirit baptism as a distinct reality from water baptism can be seen in the analogy of circumcision. The Word of God tells us that circumcision was instituted by God as a sign and seal of his covenant with Abraham: 'and he received the sign of circumcision, a seal of the righteousness of the faith which he had while uncircumcised' (Rom. 4:11). Martyn Lloyd–Jones gives this explanation of the meaning of circumcision:

> What, then, are the reasons why circumcision was ever given? First, circumcision was an outward sign given to Abraham as a seal of the righteousness which he had received fourteen years before. Now to 'seal' means to authenticate. This is illustrated elsewhere in the Scriptures. You remember that we are told in John 6, verse 27 'for him hath God the Father sealed'. All commentators are agreed that statement refers to our Lord's baptism, and it means that at His baptism He was publicly sealed with the sign of the descent of the Holy Spirit in the form of a dove upon Him. The word 'seal' is used in exactly the same way in referring to the Holy Spirit in Ephesians 1: 13, 14, 'In whom also after that ye believed (or having believed), ye were sealed with that Holy Spirit of promise, which is the earnest of our inheritance until the redemption of the purchased possession, unto the praise of His glory.' The Holy Spirit seals to us God's promise of our ultimate redemption and of our receiving our great inheritance in glory. Having the Holy Spirit I know that all that God promises to me is already mine in a very real sense. It is sealed to me. What the Apostle is saying here is that in the same way circumcision was given to Abraham as a sign to authenticate the imputation of righteousness to him fourteen years before.
>
> In other words the teaching is, that circumcision of itself did not do anything to Abraham. The real reason for it was that Abraham should have the promise made sure to him; it was to seal it to him. And so we are right in saying that circumcision played no part in Abraham's justification. Indeed it is exactly the other way round. Justification is the basis upon which circumcision is given.[79]

Circumcision was meant to be a sign and a seal. It was the outward sign of an inward reality of faith in Abraham's heart, and a seal to him of the promise of God. Romans 4:9–12 makes it clear that circumcision was not the *cause* of Abraham's regeneration and justification. He had been justified by faith *before* he was circumcised. The argument of Paul in Romans 4 is that forgiveness and acceptance with God come solely by faith independent of circumcision. At the time of Christ the Jews had perverted the meaning of circumcision, teaching that it was the effectual cause of salvation. Paul shows the fallacy of this, not only in the example of Abraham, but by drawing a distinction between outward physical circumcision and the inner spiritual circumcision accomplished by the Spirit:

> For he is not a Jew who is one outwardly; neither is circumcision that which is outward in the flesh. But he is a Jew who is one inwardly; and circumcision is that which is of the heart, by the Spirit, not by the letter; and his praise is not from men, but from God (Rom. 2:28–29).

It was not physical circumcision that made a person a true Jew, but a spiritual circumcision of the heart. As Paul points out, it is possible to be physically yet not spiritually circumcised. In Jeremiah, the prophet records an unusual observation from the Lord regarding the spiritual condition of many of the Israelites:

> 'Behold, the days are coming,' declares the Lord, 'that I will punish all who are circumcised and yet uncircumcised— Egypt, and Judah, and Edom, and the sons of Ammon, and Moab, and all those inhabiting the desert who clip the hair on their temples; for all the nations are uncircumcised, and all the house of Israel are uncircumcised of heart' (Jer. 9:25–26).

What a poignant description—circumcised in the flesh and yet uncircumcised of heart. The Lord is putting Judah in the same category as the uncircumcised heathen nations around her. Israel had a profession but no reality. The Old Testament exhorted the Jews to circumcise their hearts (demonstrating that the physical rite of circumcision was symbolic) and pointed them to the need for an inward, spiritual circumcision:

> Circumcise then your heart, and stiffen your neck no more...The Lord your God will circumcise your heart and the heart of your descendants, to love the Lord your God with all your heart and with all your soul, in order that you may live...Circumcise yourselves to the Lord and remove the foreskins of your heart (Deut. 10:16; 30:6; Jer. 4:4).

What was true for the Jew is also true for the Christian. Simply substitute the word 'Christian' for 'Jew' and the word 'baptism' for 'circumcision' in Romans 2:28–29:

> For he is not a *Christian* who is one outwardly; neither is *baptism* that which is outward in the flesh. But he is a *Christian* who is one inwardly; and *baptism* is that which is of the heart, by the Spirit, not by the letter; and his praise is not from men, but from God.

John Calvin offers the following explanation of the relationship of circumcision to baptism:

> When the Lord commands Abraham to observe circumcision, he previously states that he will be a God to him and his descendants (Gen. 17:7, 10)...The promise of eternal life is contained in these words as Christ interprets them...But the first access to God, the first entry into immortal life, is the forgiveness of sins. Accordingly, this corresponds to the promise of baptism that we shall be cleansed. Afterward, the Lord covenants with Abraham that he should walk before him in uprightness and innocence of heart (Gen. 17:1). This applies to mortification, or regeneration...Moses more clearly explains elsewhere, when exhorting the Israelite people to circumcise the foreskin of their heart to the Lord (Deut. 10:16), that circumcision is the sign of mortification...As

God, when he adopts the posterity of Abraham as his people, commands them to be circumcised, so Moses declares that they ought to be circumcised in heart, explaining the true meaning of this carnal circumcision (Deut 30:6)...We have, therefore, a spiritual promise given to the patriarchs in circumcision such as is given us in baptism, since it represented for them forgiveness of sins and mortification of flesh. Moreover, as we have been taught that Christ is the foundation of baptism, in whom both these reside, so it is also evident that he is the foundation of circumcision.[80]

The Jews believed that physical circumcision made one a child of God, but Paul insists that there must be a spiritual circumcision of the heart by the Holy Spirit. Physical baptism will not bring about the new birth. That can only be accomplished as we are recreated within by the Holy Spirit. Charles Hodge makes this comment:

God is a Spirit, and He requires those who worship Him, to worship Him in spirit and in truth. External rites are declared to be nothing. 'He is not a Jew, which is one outwardly; neither is that circumcision, which is outward in the flesh: but he is a Jew, which is one inwardly; and circumcision is that of the heart, in the spirit, and not in the letter; whose praise is not of men, but of God.' (Rom. ii. 28, 29). This is not merely a fact, but a principle. What St. Paul here says of circumcision and of Jews, may be said, and is substantially said by St. Peter in reference to baptism and Christianity. A man who is a Christian outwardly only, is not a Christian; and the baptism which saves, is not the washing of the body with water, but the conversion of the soul (I Peter iii. 21). The idea that a man's state before God depends on anything external, on birth, on membership in any visible organization, or on any outward rite or ceremony, is utterly abhorrent to the religion of the Bible.[81]

Baptism in our New Testament dispensation is to be a sign

and seal of the spiritual transformation that has taken place in the heart of the convert. It is a public testimony of the washing from sin and new life given. Spiritual circumcision and its relationship to baptism is explained by Paul in Colossians:

> In Him you were also circumcised with a circumcision made without hands, in the removal of the body of the flesh by the circumcision of Christ; having been buried with Him in baptism, in which you were also raised up with Him through faith in the working of God, who raised Him from the dead. And when you were dead in your transgressions and the uncircumcision of your flesh, He made you alive together with Him, having forgiven us all our transgressions, having canceled out the certificate of debt consisting of decrees against us and which was hostile to us; and He has taken it out of the way, having nailed it to the cross (Col. 2:11–14).

True circumcision is what Paul calls the removal of the body of flesh. Baptism is a picture of the identification of the believer with Christ in his burial. The old man dies and the individual is raised to newness of life, made 'alive together with Him.' This all speaks of regeneration. Baptism and circumcision here are not physical rites but the spiritual work of the Holy Spirit. The new Christian then submits to water baptism as a public testimony to his identification with Christ and spiritual transformation. As Charles Hodge points out:

> It is plain that baptism cannot be the ordinary means of regeneration, or the channel of conveying in the first instance the benefits of redemption to the souls of men, because, in the case of adults, faith and repentance are the conditions of baptism. But faith and repentance, according to the Scriptures, are the fruits of regeneration. He who exercises repentance towards God and faith in our Lord Jesus Christ is in a state of salvation before baptism and therefore in a state of regeneration. Regeneration consequently precedes baptism, and cannot be its effect, according to the ordinance

of God. That the Apostles did require the profession of faith and repentance before baptism, cannot be denied. This is plain, not only from their recorded practice but also from the nature of the ordinance. Baptism is a profession of faith in the Father, and the Son, and the Holy Spirit; not of a faith to be obtained through the ordinance, but of a faith already entertained. When the Eunuch applied to Philip for baptism, he said: 'If thou believest with all thine heart thou mayest.' Of those who heard Peter's sermon on the day of Pentecost it is said, 'they that gladly received his word were baptized' (Acts ii. 41).[82]

As noted, Abraham was justified long before he was circumcised. In the same way, a Christian receives an inner Spirit baptism before the actual rite of water baptism is applied. This is further illustrated in the first chapter of John:

> But as many as received Him, to them He gave the right to become children of God, even to those who believe in His name, who were born not of blood, nor of the will of the flesh, nor of the will of man, but of God (Jn. 1: 12–13).

John is speaking about the new birth. He says that it is directly related to receiving and believing on Jesus. The new birth is not dependent on water baptism but on a work of the Spirit which results in the receiving of Jesus Christ into one's life. Regeneration can never be disassociated from a personal relationship with Jesus Christ himself.

Romans 6:3–5

One of the passages of scripture often used in support of baptismal regeneration is Romans 6:3–5. It reads as follows:

> Or do you not know that all of us who have been baptized into Christ Jesus have been baptized into His death? Therefore we have been buried with Him through baptism into death, in

order that as Christ was raised from the dead through the glory of the Father, so we too might walk in newness of life. For if we have become united with Him in the likeness of His death, certainly we shall be also in the likeness of His resurrection.

These verses do speak of baptism. But when scripture uses the term 'baptism' it always assumes Spirit baptism to be the underlying reality. The apostle Peter makes this clear when he says, 'And corresponding to that, baptism now saves you— not the removal of dirt from the flesh, but an appeal to God for a good conscience—through the resurrection of Jesus Christ' (I Pet. 3:2 I). Peter is careful to warn his readers against the mistaken notion that salvation is derived simply from the application of water to physical flesh. He specifically says 'not the removal of dirt from the flesh.' He associates baptism with 'an appeal to God for a good conscience through the resurrection of Jesus Christ.' There is obviously more to be understood by the term 'baptism' here than the administering of water. Matthew Henry brings this out in these comments on this passage:

> Noah's salvation in the ark upon the water prefigured the salvation of all good Christians in the church by baptism; that temporal salvation by the ark was a type, the antitype whereunto is the eternal salvation of believers by baptism, to prevent mistakes about which the apostle declares what he means by saving baptism; not the outward ceremony of washing with water, which, in itself, does no more than put away the filth of the flesh, but it is that baptism wherein there is a faithful answer or restipulation of a resolved good conscience, engaging to believe in, and be entirely devoted to, God, the Father, Son, and Holy Ghost, renouncing at the same time the flesh, the world, and the devil. The baptismal covenant, made and kept, will certainly save us. Washing is the visible sign; this is the thing signified.
>
> The apostle shows that the efficacy of baptism to salvation

depends not upon the work done, but upon the resurrection of Christ, which supposes his death, and is the foundation of our faith and hope, to which we are rendered conformable by dying to sin, and rising again to holiness and newness of life..... The external participation of baptism will save no man without an answerable good conscience and conversation. There must be the answer of a good conscience towards God.[83]

The point of this Romans 6 is to establish that those who are baptized into Christ are freed from sin to walk in newness of life as slaves of righteousness (Rom. 6:4, 17–18). Again, this is not something effected through water baptism but by a supernatural work of the Holy Spirit in the heart of a man or woman.

When Spirit baptism takes place, an individual is joined to and identified with Christ in his death, burial and resurrection. The result of this union is a completely changed life. It is impossible for one who is a true Christian to continue to live under the domination of sin as a way of life. Rom. 6:1–2 says:

> What shall we say then? Are we to continue in sin that grace might increase? May it never be! How shall we who died to sin still live in it?

1 John 3:9 says, 'No one who is born of God practices sin, because His seed abides in him; and he cannot sin, because he is born of God.'

Romans 6:4 tells us that the person who has been united to Jesus Christ will walk in 'newness of life.' This person will not live or abide in sin. However a person *can* be baptized with water and still continue to live in sin, but the person who is baptized by the Holy Spirit into Christ will not *practice* sin.

This is not to deny the importance of water baptism. But it *must* be preceded by the cleansing and regenerating power of the Holy Spirit. Water baptism is an outward picture of an inward work of grace. It does not bring about the new birth but is a testimony to it. The Reformers, Huldrych Zwingli and John Hooper make clear the place of baptism with these comments:

Huldrych Zwingli: Water–baptism is a ceremonial sign with which salvation is not indissolubly connected...The inward baptism of the Spirit is the work of teaching which God does in our hearts and the calling with which he comforts and assures our hearts in Christ. And this baptism none can give save God alone. Without it, none can be saved–though it is quite possible to be saved without the baptism of external...immersion. The proof of this is that the murderer on the cross was externally neither taught nor baptized, and yet he was saved. It follows that the one necessary thing which saves those of us who hear the Gospel is faith, or trust, and this faith none can implant within us save God alone...External baptism of water cannot effect spiritual cleansing. Hence water–baptism is nothing but an external ceremony, that is, an outward sign that we are incorporated and engrafted into the Lord Jesus Christ and pledged to live to him and to follow him. And in Jesus Christ neither circumcision nor uncircumcision avails anything, but a new creature, the living of a new life (Gal. 6), so it is not baptism that saves us but a new life.[84]

John Hooper: Although baptism be a sacrament to be received and honourably used of all men, yet it sanctifieth no man. And such as attribute the remission of sin unto the external sign, doth offend...This new life cometh not, until such a time as Christ be known and received. Now, to put on Christ is to live a new life. Such as be baptized must remember, that penance (repentance) and faith preceded this external sign, and in Christ the purgation was inwardly obtained, before the external sign was given. So that there is two kinds of baptism, and both necessary: the one interior, which is the cleansing of the heart, the drawing of the Father, the operation of the Holy Ghost: and this baptism is in man, when he believeth and trusteth that Christ is the only author of his salvation...Then is the exterior sign added, not to purge the heart, but to confirm, manifest, and open unto the world that this child is God's...Likewise no man should condemn nor neglect this exterior sign, for the commandment's sake: though it have no power to purge from sin, yet it confirmeth the purgation of sin, and the act of itself pleaseth God, for because the receivers thereof obey the will of his commandment.[85]

With this in mind let us look at the teaching of Jesus in his dialogue with Nicodemus.

John 3:3–5

Jesus answered and said to him [Nicodemus], 'Truly, truly, I say to you, unless one is born again, he cannot see the kingdom of God.' Nicodemus said to him, 'How can a man be born when he is old? He cannot enter a second time into his mother's womb and be born, can he?' Jesus answered, 'Truly, truly, I say to you, unless one is born of water and the Spirit, he cannot enter into the kingdom of God.'

Jesus says we must be born again or we will not enter the kingdom of heaven. He tells Nicodemus that a man must be 'born of water and the Spirit.' What did he mean? Did Jesus mean water baptism here? Three reasons suggest that he did not. Firstly, the Bible teaches that water baptism does not save. Secondly, Jesus is speaking to Nicodemus, who is a Jew. Christian baptism had not yet been instituted. And thirdly, because Jesus is speaking to Nicodemus, the term must be interpreted in context. The term 'water' had a certain significance to Nicodemus, who was a learned Jew, a leading, if not *the* leading teacher in Israel (Jn. 3:10). Jesus upbraids Nicodemus for not understanding his teaching. In so doing he is suggesting that the meaning of his teaching is clear in the

Old Testament. What significance would the term 'water' have had for Nicodemus? John Murray's comments on John 3:5 are very helpful at this point:

> Now what religious idea would we expect to be conveyed to the mind of Nicodemus by the use of the word water? Of course, the idea associated with the religious use of water in the Old Testament and in that religious tradition and practice which provided the very context of Nicodemus' life and profession! And that simply means the religious import of water in the Old Testament, in the rites of Judaism, and in contemporary practice. When we say this, there is one answer. The religious use of water, that is to say, the religiously symbolic meaning of water, pointed in one direction, and that direction is purification. All the relevant considerations would conspire to convey to Nicodemus that message. And that message would be focused in his mind in one central thought, the indispensable necessity of purification for entrance into the kingdom of God.
>
> In the Old Testament water often signified washing and purifying from the pollution of sin (cf. Psalm 5 I: 2,3; Isa. 1:16; Jer. 33:8; Ezek. 36:25; Zech. 13: 1)....John 3:5 sets forth the two aspects from which the new birth must be viewed—it purges away the defilement of our hearts and it recreates in newness of life. The two elements of this text—'born of water' and 'born of the Spirit' correspond to the two elements of the Old Testament counterpart: 'Then will I sprinkle clean water upon you, and ye shall be clean: from all your filthiness, and from all your idols, will I cleanse you. A new heart also will I give you, and a new spirit will I put within you: and I will take away the stony heart out of your flesh, and I will give you an heart of flesh' (Ezek. 36:25,26). This passage we may properly regard as the Old Testament parallel to John 3:5, and there is neither reason nor warrant for placing any other interpretation upon 'born of water' than that of Ezek. 36:25: 'Then will I sprinkle clean water upon you, and ye shall be clean.'[86]

To Nicodemus the term 'water' would have meant cleansing from the guilt and pollution of sin. In John 3:5 therefore the term 'water' refers to this spiritual cleansing. Paul says, similarly, in Titus 3:5: 'He saved us, not on the basis of deeds which we have done in righteousness, but according to His mercy, by the washing of regeneration and renewing by the Holy Spirit.' This 'washing' takes place through the work of Christ on our behalf: 'To Him who has loved us and washed (loosed)us from our sins by His blood' (Rev. 1:5).

The passage in Ezekiel 36 is a prophecy of the New Covenant effected through our Mediator and High Priest, the Lord Jesus Christ. These verses are quoted in Hebrews 8, referring to the inauguration of the New Covenant through Christ. So regeneration, as it was prophesied in the Old Testament, has direct application to a relationship with Jesus Christ and his work of atonement on the cross.

The basis for entering the kingdom of God is washing, cleansing, and purification from the guilt and defilement of our sin through the blood of Jesus Christ. The agent by which we are actually regenerated is the Spirit of God. He brings us into the kingdom of God cleansed and made new through the blood of Jesus and the sovereign power of regeneration. This is further amplified in John 3:14–16:

> And as Moses lifted up the serpent in the wilderness, even so must the Son of Man be lifted up; that whoever believes may in Him have eternal life. For God so loved the world, that He gave His only begotten Son, that whoever believes in Him should not perish, but have eternal life.

In Moses' day a bronze serpent was attached to a wooden pole and then lifted up so that those who looked at it would not die. In the same way, God's Son was to be lifted up—nailed to a cross—to die for the sin of the world. God so loved the world that he gave his only begotten Son, that those who believe in him and the sufficiency of his blood sacrifice would not perish eternally, but possess eternal life. Life, new and eternal, is

found in a relationship with Jesus Christ. Jesus said 'I am the
way and the truth and *the life*' (Jn. 14:6). Those who receive
him are given the power to become the children of God, that
is, they are regenerated (Jn. 1:12). As D.A. Carson puts it:

> What spared the Israelites from the mortal threat of the
> desert snakes was God's grace; the means was the bronze
> snake. But we must say more than that about Jesus. The
> Father has granted the Son to have life in himself (Jn. 5:26);
> he himself is the resurrection and the life (Jn. 11:25), and
> those who believe have life *in him*. Here then is the frankest
> answer to Nicodemus' question, 'How can this happen?' (v.
> 9). The Kingdom of God is seen or entered, new birth is
> experienced, and eternal life begins, through the saving
> cross–work of Christ, received by faith.[87]

In the context of John 3 regeneration has nothing to do with
water but with the Spirit baptism by which we are united to
Christ, cleansed from sin and given a new heart. Calvin
stresses this point when he says:

> Paul did not mean to signify that our cleansing and salvation
> are accomplished by water, or that water contains in itself the
> power to cleanse, regenerate, and renew; nor that here is the
> cause of salvation, but only that in this sacrament are
> received the knowledge and certainty of such gifts...Indeed,
> baptism promises us no other purification than through the
> sprinkling of Christ's blood, which is represented by means of
> water from the resemblance to cleansing and washing. Who,
> therefore, may say that we are cleansed by this water which
> attests with certainty that Christ's blood is our true and only
> laver? Thus, the surest argument to refute the self–deception
> of those who attribute everything to the power of the water
> can be sought in the meaning of baptism itself, which draws us
> away, not only from the visible element which meets our eyes,
> but from all other means, that it may fasten our minds upon
> Christ alone.[88]

So, 'How can I be born again?' Scripture always places before us a relationship with Christ as the ultimate answer to every spiritual need we have. Regeneration is the exclusive work of God but cannot be separated from the preaching of the gospel or from union with Christ, repentance, faith or conversion. As Berkhof states: 'The moment when we are united with Christ is also the moment of our regeneration and justification.'[89] And Dabney states that our union with Christ is accomplished by the Spirit of God through faith: 'The instrumental bond of the union is evidently faith—i.e., when the believer exercises faith, the union begins.'[90] Thus, regeneration, union with Christ, repentance, faith and conversion are inseparable. John Murray says:

> Regeneration in its restricted sense...must never be abstracted from its context. The context of regeneration in the restricted sense is one that has no meaning apart from the truth of the gospel addressed to and engaging our consciousness. Regeneration takes place in connection with the effectual call; it pushes itself into consciousness in the responses of faith and repentance. It has no relevance except as it is concomitant with these other aspects of the *ordo salutis*...Regeneration must not be separated from calling on the one hand and faith and repentance on the other.[91]

~ 9 ~

Repentance

Unless you repent, you will...perish (Luke 13:3)

Repentance is a major emphasis in the teaching of the New Testament. Jesus came 'to call sinners to repentance' (Mt. 9:13) and his gospel presentation included both repentance and faith: 'The time is fulfilled, and the kingdom of God is at hand; repent and believe the gospel' (Mk. 1:15). He taught that repentance is necessary for salvation: 'Unless you repent, you will...perish' (Lk. 13:3), and he commanded that it be preached throughout the world as part of the Great Commission: 'that repentance for the forgiveness of sins should be proclaimed in His name to all the nations' (Lk.24:47). Repentance was also the hallmark of the preaching of John the Baptist (Mt. 3:1–8) and of the apostles Peter and Paul.

Peter taught that repentance and conversion are necessary for salvation: 'Repent therefore and return, that your sins might be wiped away' (Acts 3:19); that Christ's purpose in ascending to heaven was to grant repentance and forgiveness of sins: 'He is the one whom God exalted to His right hand as a Prince and a Savior, to grant repentance to Israel, and forgiveness of sins' (Acts 5:31); and that 'God is not wishing for any to perish but for all to come to repentance' (2 Pet. 3:9). Paul's gospel consisted of 'repentance toward God and faith in our Lord Jesus Christ' (Acts 20:21). He preached to the Gentiles that 'God is now declaring to men that all everywhere should repent' (Acts 17:30) and therefore 'they

should repent and turn to God, performing deeds appropriate
to repentance' (Acts 26:20). Clearly, scripture teaches that
repentance is part of the human response to the gospel of God
and is necessary for salvation. As Jesus said: 'Unless you
repent you will...perish' (Lk. 13:3). Apart from repentance
one cannot exercise saving faith.

Repentance and faith are separate concepts. But while they
are distinct and different, we cannot separate them in the
application and appropriation of salvation. True faith always
involves repentance and true repentance always involves
faith. Both to be preached when calling men to Christ. John
Calvin taught that there could be no separating them:

> Even though we have taught in part how to possess Christ,
> and how through it we enjoy his benefits, this would still
> remain obscure if we did not add an explanation of the effects
> we feel. With good reason, the sum of the gospel is held to
> consist in repentance and the forgiveness of sins (Luke 24:47;
> Acts 5:31). Any discussion of faith, therefore, that omitted
> these two topics would be barren and mutilated and well–
> nigh useless...Surely no one can embrace the grace of the
> gospel without betaking himself from the errors of his past
> life into the right way, and applying his whole effort to the
> practice of repentance.
>
> Can true repentance stand apart from faith? Not at all. But
> even though they cannot be separated, they ought to be
> distinguished.[92]

Zwingli further expresses the emphasis of the Reformation
on repentance:

> The second part of the gospel, then, is repentance: not that
> which takes place for a time, but that which makes a man who
> knows himself blush and be ashamed of his old life, for one
> reason because he sees it ought to be altogether foreign to a
> Christian to waste away in those sins from which he rejoiced
> to believe that he had been delivered...Therefore when Christ

and John and the Apostles preach, saying, 'Repent,' they are simply calling us to a new life quite unlike our life before; and those who had undertaken to enter upon this were marked by an initiatory sacrament, baptism to wit, by which they give public testimony that they were going to enter upon a new life.[93]

Martin Bucer likewise stresses the necessity for repentance:

It is a quality of the Kingdom of Christ that in it the repentance of sinners must always be preached. Hence where the kingdom of Christ has truly been received, there it is necessary that the sins of all be severely rebuked, that men may give themselves up completely to the kingship of Christ in order to be cleansed from their sins and endowed with the spirit of righteousness...Thus it is a hollow mockery that those who do not make a wholehearted effort to do the things that are pleasing to the heavenly Father should declare themselves citizens and members of the Kingdom of Christ.[94]

The seventeenth century puritan, Thomas Watson, says:

Repentance is of such importance that there is no being saved without it...It is a great duty incumbent upon Christians solemnly to repent and turn unto God...That religion which is not built upon this foundation must needs fall to the ground.

Repentance is a grace required under the gospel. Some think it legal; but the first sermon that Christ preached, indeed, the first word of his sermon, was 'Repent' (*Matt. 4.17*). And his farewell that he left when he was going to ascend was that 'repentance should be preached in his name' (*Luke 22.47*)...Repentance is not arbitrary. It is not left to our choice whether or not we will repent, but it is an indispensable command. God has enacted a law in the High Court of heaven that no sinner shall be saved except the repenting sinner, and he will not break his own law.

Some bless themselves that they have a stock of knowledge,

but what is knowledge good for without repentance? It is better to mortify one sin than to understand all mysteries. Impure speculatists do but resemble Satan transformed into an angel of light. Learning and a bad heart is like a fair face with a cancer in the breast. Knowledge without repentance will be but a torch to light men to hell.[95]

In scripture, repentance is placed on an equal footing with faith in the proclamation of the gospel. The call of the gospel is a call to repentance and faith, not simply to faith. Repentance does not save but one cannot exercise saving faith, appropriate Christ or experience salvation, apart from biblical repentance. Some take exception to this, arguing that repentance is a fruit of faith. However, most Reformed theologians agree with this teaching. For example, Berkhof teaches that repentance and conviction of sin *precede* faith rather than being the fruit of it:

There is no doubt that, logically, repentance and the knowledge of sin precedes the faith that yields to Christ in trusting love.[96]

And John Murray says:

The question has been discussed: which is prior, faith or repentance? It is an unnecessary question and the insistence that one is prior to the other is futile. There is no priority. The faith that is unto salvation is a penitent faith and the repentance that is unto life is a believing repentance...It is impossible to disentangle faith and repentance. Saving faith is permeated with repentance and repentance is permeated with faith.[97]

The Westminster Confession emphasizes the importance of preaching repentance as well as faith:

Repentance unto life is an evangelical grace, the doctrine

whereof is to be preached by every minister of the gospel, as well as that of faith in Christ. By it a sinner, out of sight and sense, not only of danger, but also of filthiness and odiousness of his sins, as contrary to the holy nature and righteous law of God, and upon the apprehension of his mercy in Christ to such as are penitent, so grieves for and hates his sins, as to turn from them all unto God, purposing and endeavoring to walk with him in all the ways of his commandments.[98]

R.L. Dabney comments:

The manner in which faith and repentance are coupled together in Scripture plainly shows that, as faith is implicitly present in repentance, so repentance is implicitly in faith.[99]

The Westminster Confession and most Reformed theologians teach that repentance is not a fruit of faith but of regeneration. More importantly, the teaching that repentance is a fruit of faith is not the teaching of scripture. As with faith, it is described equally with faith as a gift of God and the fruit of the sovereign work of the Holy Spirit in regeneration. Repentance and faith define what it means to turn to God in Christ for salvation. It is imperative that we adequately emphasize *both* of these doctrines. One cannot come to Christ to receive imputed righteousness, forgiveness and eternal life apart from faith *and* repentance. We must maintain a balance in our teaching and preaching. We dare not minimize a doctrine that scripture emphasizes, especially when it relates to salvation. Unfortunately, this is happening in much of evangelicalism today. There is much teaching on faith to the diminishing of the importance of repentance. And this is not a new problem. As Dabney observed:

Repentance unto Life is an evangelical grace, the doctrine whereof is to be preached by every minister of the gospel, as well as that of faith in Christ (Conf. xv.1). The brevity, and in some cases neglect, with which this prominent subject is treated by many systems, is surprising and reprehensible.[100]

We need to stress repentance as much as faith because apart from repentance a man cannot exercise saving faith.

What then is repentance? The Greek word for repentance is *metanoia* which literally means a change of mind; a change of mind toward sin whereby man comes to detest his sin and purposes to forsake it. John Calvin comments:

> The Hebrew word for 'repentance' is derived from conversion or return; the Greek word, from change of mind or of intention. And the thing itself corresponds closely to the etymology of both words. *The meaning is that, departing from ourselves, we turn to God,* and having taken off our former mind, we put on a new. On this account, in my judgment, repentance can thus be well defined: *it is the turning of our life to God...*When we call it a 'turning of life to God,' we require a transformation, not only in outward works, but in the soul itself. Only when it puts off its old nature does it bring forth the fruits of works in harmony with its renewal. The prophet, wishing to express this change, bids whom he calls to repentance to *get themselves a new heart* (Ezek. 18:31).
>
> Outward uprightness of life is not the chief point of repentance, for God looks into men's hearts. Whoever is moderately versed in Scripture will understand by himself...that when we have to deal with God nothing is achieved unless we begin from the *inner disposition of the heart* (emphasis mine).[101]

John DeWitt says:

> Repentance is the first conscious step in a person's experience of the divine grace, the entrance for all believers into life, hope, and salvation...Repentance—the repentance of which the Scriptures speak as a godly sorrow, the repentance which is unto life—is not only a persuasion of

sinfulness, but it is also, and very distinctly, a turning from sin...Everywhere the Word of God reminds us that repentance is not simply honesty with oneself, or even the open confession of one's sins; it must also lead to a *forsaking* of them. If it does not do that, if it is only the fear of punishment and of hell, only a trembling before the just judgment of God, without at the same time the purposing to turn away from sin and to undertake a new obedience to God, then it is not repentance at all.[102]

In his commentary on the Westminster Confession, A.A. Hodge gives these important observations on repentance:

> The essence of repentance consists...in our actual turning from all sin unto God. This is that practical turning or 'conversion' from sin unto God, which is the instant and necessary consequence of regeneration. It is a voluntary forsaking of sin as evil and hateful, with sincere sorrow, humiliation, and confession; and a turning unto God as our reconciled Father, in the exercise of implicit faith in the merits and assisting grace of Christ...Repentance unto life can only be exercised by a soul after, and in consequence of, its regeneration by the Holy Spirit. God regenerates; and we, in the exercise of the new gracious ability thus given, repent...If genuine, it infallibly springs from regeneration and leads to eternal life.[103]

And Charles Hodge states:

> Hence it is that repentance is the burden of evangelical preaching...Repentance...is the great, immediate, and pressing duty of all who hear the gospel. They are called upon to forsake their sins, and return unto God through Jesus Christ. The neglect of this duty is the rejection of salvation. For, as we have seen, unless we repent we must perish...Though repentance is a duty, it is no less the gift of God.[104]

The importance of turning from sin and its relationship to forgiveness and conversion is seen in the following scriptures:

Seek the LORD while He may be found; call upon Him while He is near. *Let the wicked forsake his way,* and the unrighteous man his thoughts; and let him *return to the LORD,* and He will have compassion on him; and to our God, for He will abundantly pardon (Is. 55:6–7).

And a Redeemer will come to Zion, and to those who *turn from transgression* in Jacob, declares the Lord (Is. 59:20).

Say to them, 'As I live!' declares the Lord GOD, 'I take no pleasure in the death of the wicked, but rather that *the wicked turn from his way and live.* Turn back, turn back from your evil ways! Why then will you die, O house of Israel?' (Ez. 33:11).

Therefore I will judge you, O house of Israel, each according to his conduct, declares the Lord GOD. *Repent and turn away from all your transgressions,* so that iniquity may not become a stumbling block to you (Ez. 18:30).

Therefore say to the house of Israel, Thus says the Lord GOD, '*Repent and turn away from your idols, and turn your faces away from all your abominations'* (Ez.14:6).

For you first, God raised up His Servant, and sent Him to bless you by *turning every one of you from your wicked ways*(Acts 3:26).

And the hand of the Lord was with them, and a large number who *believed turned to the Lord* (Acts 11:21).

We are also men of the same nature as you, and preach the gospel to you in order that you *should turn from these vain things to a living God,* Who made the heaven and the earth and the sea, and all that is in them (Acts 14:15).

To open their eyes so that they may *turn from darkness to light and from the dominion of Satan to God,* in order that they may receive forgiveness of sins and an inheritance among those who have been sanctified by faith in Me' (Acts 26:18)

But kept declaring both to those of Damascus first, and also at Jerusalem and then throughout all the region of Judea, and even to the Gentiles, that *they should repent and turn to*

God, performing deeds appropriate to repentance (Acts 26:20).

For they themselves report about us what kind of a reception we had with you, and how you *turned to God from idols* to serve a living and true God (1 Thes. 1:9).

Repentance means turning from sin. It does not mean a mere acknowledgment of sin or remorse, but a *turning from* it with a purpose to forsake it altogether. Sin is defined by the law. As we have seen, the law relates to God as a person and to his will. And repentance therefore relates to God as well as to issues of behavior. Paul preached 'repentance towards God'(Acts 20:21), and that men must 'bring forth fruits meet for repentance' (Acts 26:20). If man is to enter into salvation he must also turn from self–will and self–rule and submit his life to Christ as Lord and First Love, in addition to turning from behavioral sins. A.W. Pink sums it up in these words:

In repentance sin is the thing to be repented of and sin is a transgression of the law (1 John 3:4). And the first and chief thing required by the law is supreme love to God. Therefore, the lack of supreme love to God, the heart's disaffection for His character and rebellion against Him (Rom. 8:7) is our great wickedness, of which we have to repent.

What is sin? Sin is saying...I disallow His (God's) right to govern me...I am going to be lord of myself. Sin is rebellion against the Majesty of heaven...The language of every sinner's heart is, I care not what God requires, I am going to have my own way. I care not what be God's claims upon me, I refuse to submit to His authority...The Lord Jesus taught and constantly pressed the same truth. His call was 'Repent ye and believe the gospel' (Mark 1:15). The gospel cannot be savingly believed until there is genuine repentance.

When the gospel first comes to the sinner it finds him in a state of apostasy from God, both as sovereign Ruler and as our supreme good, neither obeying and glorifying Him, nor enjoying and finding satisfaction in Him. Hence the demand for 'repentance toward God' before 'faith toward our Lord Jesus Christ' (Acts 20:21). True repentance toward God removes this dissatisfaction of our minds and hearts toward Him, under both these characters. In saving repentance the whole soul turns to Him and says: I have been a disloyal and rebellious creature. I have scorned Thy high authority and most rightful law. I will live no longer thus. I desire and determine with all my might to serve and obey Thee as my only Lord. I subject myself unto Thee, to submit to Thy will...Repentance...is the perception that God has the right to rule and govern me, and of my refusal to submit unto Him...As the Holy Spirit sets before me the loveliness of the divine character, as I am enabled to discern the exalted excellency of God, then I begin to perceive that to which He is justly entitled, namely, the homage of my heart, the unrestricted love of my soul, the complete surrender of my whole being unto Him.

Many are the scriptures which set forth this truth, that there must be a forsaking of sin before God will pardon offenders...He must be crowned Lord of all or He will not be Lord at all. There must be the complete heart renunciation of all that stands in competition with Him. He will brook no rival...Thus repentance is the negative side of conversion. Conversion is a whole–hearted turning unto God, but there cannot be a turning unto, without a turning from. Sin must be forsaken ere we draw nigh unto the Holy One. As it is written, 'Ye turned to God from idols to serve (live for) the living and true God' (1 Thes. 1:9).[105]

This emphasis on repentance has important implications in understanding the Reformation teaching of *faith alone*. When we say we are saved and justified by faith alone we understand that term faith to mean a repentant–faith. The quotations cited from the various Reformers and Reformed theologians affirm this. Repentance is an essential element of biblical faith. In order to turn *to Christ* one must turn *from* sin. Repentance is a gift of God and not a work. It does not save, and is not the basis of one's acceptance with God, but an individual cannot be saved without it. The reason being that one cannot appropriate the person of Christ, who is our justification before God, apart from repentance. This truth bears repeating: Salvation is more than deliverance from the guilt and condemnation of sin in justification and therefore of hell. It includes deliverance from sin as a ruling power in one's life. In the preaching of the gospel this fact must be emphasized: Coming to Christ for salvation will mean a turning from sin and idols or Christ cannot be received. As Jonathan Edwards observes:

> The apostasy of man summarily consists in departing from the true God, to idols; forsaking his Creator and setting up other things in his room...The gods which a natural man worships, instead of the God that made him, are himself and the world...When we say that natural man are not willing to come to Christ, it is not meant that they are not willing to be delivered from hell; for without doubt, no natural man is willing to go to hell. Nor is it meant, that they are not willing that Christ should keep them from going to hell. Without doubt, natural men under awakenings often greatly desire this. But this does not argue that they are willing to come to Christ: for, not withstanding their desire to be delivered from hell, their hearts do not close with Christ, but are averse to him...They are not willing to take Christ as he is; they would fain divide him. There are some things in him that they like, and others that they greatly dislike; but consider him as he is, and he is offered to them in the gospel, and they are not willing to accept Christ; for in doing so, they must of necessity part with all their sins; they must sell the world, and part with their own righteousness. But they had rather, for the present, run the venture of going to hell, than do that...He is a Savior appointed of God; he anointed him, and sent him into the world. And in performing the work of redemption, he wrought the works of God; always did those things that pleased him; and all that he does as a Savior, is to his glory.

And one great thing he aimed at in redemption, was to deliver them from their idols, and bring them to God.[106]

John Owen says:

> The repentance which, in any case, God requireth absolutely, is that which is internal and real, in sincere conversion unto himself, accompanied with the fruits meet for such repentance...A new heart and a new spirit, or real internal conversion unto God, by the grace of the covenant, is required in this repentance, as the renunciation and relinquishment of all iniquities must be the fruit of it.[107]

Repentance is commanded by God. It is a turning from all that is opposed to God as expressed in his law. We were created to love God, to live in submission to him, to worship, serve and obey him. Sin is rebellion against this purpose, loving self and the world instead. We must repent. But repentance will mean more than turning from individual *sins* in our lives. We must also deal with the root cause of sins—self. Living a life of independence from God in self–will and self–rule is sin. We must not only repent of what we *do*, but of what we *are*—self centered, self directed, independent creatures. If a person has not surrendered his heart and life to Jesus Christ as Lord he has not fully repented of sin. Charles Spurgeon makes this point in these remarks:

> Evangelical repentance is repentance of sin as sin: not of this sin nor of that, but of the whole mass. We repent of the sin of our *nature* as well as the sin of our practice. We bemoan sin within us and without us. We repent of sin itself as being an insult to God. Anything short of this is a mere surface repentance, and not a repentance which reaches to the bottom of the mischief. Repentance of the evil act, and not of the evil heart, is like men pumping water out of a leaky vessel, but forgetting to stop the leak. Some would dam up the stream, but leave the fountain still flowing; they would

remove the eruption from the skin, but leave the disease in the flesh.[108]

B.B. Warfield makes this observation:

> By repentance we are to mean, not merely sorrow for and hatred of sin, but also the inward turning away from it to God, with full purpose of new obedience. By original sin we are to mean not merely adherent but also inherent sin, not merely the sinful act of Adam imputed to us, but also the sinful state of our own souls conveyed to us by the just judgment of God. When so understood, it would seem sufficiently clear that we must 'repent of original sin.' The corruption that is derived by us from our first parents comes to us, indeed, as penalty; but it abides in us as sin, and must be looked upon as sin both by God and by enlightened conscience itself...And thus it appears, that so far from its being impossible to repent of original sin, repentance, considered in its normative sense— not as an act of turning away from this sin or that sin, but of turning from sin as such to God—is fundamentally just repentance of 'original sin.' Until we repent of original sin, we have not, properly speaking, repented in the Christian sense at all. For it is characteristic of heathen thought to look upon sin atomistically as only so many acts of sin, and at repentance also, therefore, atomistically as only so many acts of turning away from sinning; the Christian conception probes deeper and finds behind the acts of sin the sinful nature and behind the specific acts of repentance for sins the great normative act of repentance for this sinful nature. He only, then, has really repented who has perceived and felt the filthiness and odiousness of his depraved nature and has turned from it to God with a full purpose of being hereafter more conformed to his image as revealed in the face of Jesus Christ.[109]

Repentance is a turning from sin, self and the world to God in Christ. In order to turn *to* Christ, one must first turn *from* sin. This is the consistent teaching of scripture, the Reformers and

Reformed theologians who have remained true to the heritage of the Reformation. To deny or diminish the necessity for repentance is a repudiation of the gospel of scripture and of the Reformation. This brings us to a consideration of faith in the application of redemption.

~ 10 ~

Faith

*For by grace you have been saved through faith; and that not
of yourselves, it is the gift of God; not as a result of works,
that no one should boast (Ephesians 2:8-9)*

The companion truth to repentance in the divine call to
lost men and women is faith. It is the means God has
ordained for an individual to enter into salvation:

> Therefore having been justifed *by faith*, we have peace with
> God through our Lord Jesus Christ (Rom. 5:1).
> For we maintain that a man is justified *by faith* apart from
> the works of the Law (Rom. 3:28).
> Nevertheless knowing that a man is not justified by the
> works of the Law but *through faith* in Christ Jesus (Gal. 2:16).
> The righteous man shall live *by faith* (Rom. 1:17).
> For by grace you have been saved *through faith*; and that not
> of yourselves, it is the gift of God; not as a result of works, that
> no one should boast (Eph. 2:8–9).

Salvation and justification are gifts of God received by faith.
But what does scripture mean when it says we are saved and
justified *by* faith? Does it teach that faith is somehow the
grounds of our justification? No. We are not saved *by* faith but
through faith. The object of our faith is Christ. It is not faith
then, but Christ who saves. Faith is not the basis of
justification. Faith is the *means* God has ordained for
appropriating salvation by appropriating Christ himself. Joel

Beeke gives a very helpful description of the use of the Greek terms in the New Testament to describe the relationship of faith to salvation and justification:

> The Old Testament affirms that justification is 'by faith.' Of Abraham's faith Genesis 15:6 states: 'And he believed in the Lord; and he counted it to him for righteousness.'...Paul confirms in Romans 4 and Galatians 3:6–14 that the imputed (i.e. reckoned) righteousness of Genesis 15:6 is to be understood in terms of 'by or through faith.'...But the objection may be raised: Does not the preposition *eis* as used in Romans 4:5, 9, 22 (Abraham's 'faith is counted *for* righteousness...faith was reckoned to Abraham *for* righteousness...It was imputed to him *for* righteousness') imply that the act of believing is imputed to the believer for righteousness? In these verses the Greek preposition *eis* does not signify 'in the stead of,' but always means 'with a view to' or 'in order to.' It could be translated 'towards' or 'unto.' Its meaning is clear in Romans 10:10, 'with the heart man believeth *unto [eis]* righteousness'—i.e. faith moves toward and lays hold of Christ Himself.
>
> What then is the precise relationship of faith to justification? How does faith effect or accomplish the believer's justification? The answer lies in what is entailed in the preposition 'by.'...The New Testament writers commonly employ three expressions: *pistei, ek pisteos,* and *dia pisteos.* The Christian is justified 'by faith' (*pistei* or *ek pisteos*) or 'through faith' (*dia pisteos*). For example *pistei* (the dative case of the noun *pistis*) is used in Romans 3:28: 'Therefore we conclude that a man is justified *by faith* without the deeds of the law.' *Ek Pisteos* is used in Romans 5:1: 'Therefore being justified *by faith*, we have peace with God through our Lord Jesus Christ.' *Dia pisteos* is used in Ephesians 2:8: 'For by grace are ye saved *through faith*; and that not of yourselves: it is the gift of God.'
>
> Each of these three usages has its own special emphais or significance. The use of the simple dative (*pistei*) calls

attention to the necessity and importance of faith. The use of the preposition *dia* ('through' or 'by means of') describes faith as the *instrument* of justification, i.e., the means by which the righteousness of Christ is received and appropriated by the sinner unto justification. The use of the preposition *ek* ('from,' 'out of,' or 'by') describes faith as the *occasion* of justification, though never as the efficient or ultimate cause of justification.

It is critical to note that in none of these cases, nor anywhere else in Scripture, is faith (or any other grace) represented as constituting some ground of merit for justification. And this is all the more remarkable when one considers that *dia* with the accusative would mean 'on the ground of' or 'on account of.' Thus, *dia ten pisten* would convey the notion of 'on the ground of or on account of faith,' thereby making faith the meritorious reason for the believer's acceptance with God. Yet such is the precision of the Spirit's oversight of the new Testament scriptures that nowhere does any writer ever slip into using this prepositional phrase. On every occasion faith is presented as the *means* of justification. Justification by faith alone is never justification on account of faith (*propter fidem*), but always justification on account of Christ (*propter Christum*), i.e. on account of the blood–satisfaction of the Lamb of God being graciously imputed to and received by an undeserving sinner (Galatians 3:6; James 2:23). Ultimately, the ground of justification is Christ and His righteousness.

Faith is not an agent (i.e. an efficient cause), but an instrument (i.e. a means) of justification. It is the believer's sole means by which he receives justification. This means is not as mechanical as the word 'instrument' unfortunately implies; rather, this means is itself the saving work of the Holy Spirit through the Word whereby a sinner is brought into a living, personal relationship with the triune God.[110]

God has provided salvation through the Lord Jesus Christ which must be appropriated by faith. As we have seen, inherent in this faith is a turning from all human works to trust in Christ and his finished work *alone* for justification. Scripture tells us that salvation is not merited by human works of any kind (Cf. Gal. 2:16–21; Eph. 2:8–9; Tit. 3:5; Rom. 3:19–28) and any attempts to add human merit and works to justification will nullify grace and the gospel. Romans 11:6 says, 'But if it is by grace, it is no longer on the basis of works, otherwise grace is no longer grace.' And Romans 4 says that if salvation is in accordance with grace, it must be by faith, for if it is in any way related to works then faith is made void and the promise is nullified: 'For if those who are of the Law are heirs, faith is made void and the promise is nullified...For this reason it is by faith, that it might be in accordance with grace' (Rom. 4:14, 16). As they relate to justification, grace and works are anithetical. They cannot coexist. Thus, saving faith relies solely upon the person of Christ and his merits (his holy life and death on the cross) for forgiveness and acceptance with God. The Reformation teaching of *sola fide* or faith alone affirms the biblical teaching that justification is the *exclusive* work of Christ *alone* through grace *alone*. Martin Luther expresses this truth in defending his use of the word *alone* in his German translation of the scriptures:

In Romans iii, I know right well that the word *solum* was not in the Greek or Latin text...It is a fact that these four letters *s–o–l–a* are not there...At the same time...the sense of them is there and...the word belongs there if the translation is to be clear and strong. I wanted to speak German, not Latin or Greek, since I had undertaken to speak German in the translation...It is the way of the German language to add the word 'only,' in order that the word 'not' or 'no' may be more complete or clearer...I was not only relying on the nature of the languages and following that when, in Romans iii, I inserted the word *solum*, 'only,' but the text itself and the sense of St. Paul demanded it and forced it upon me. He is dealing, in that passage, with the main point of Christian doctrine, viz., that we are justified by faith in Christ, without any works of the law, and he cuts away all works so completely, as even to say that the works of the law, though it is God's law and His Word, do not help us to righteousness...But when works are so completely cut away, the meaning of it must be that faith alone justifies, and one who would speak plainly and clearly about this cutting away of all works, must say, 'Faith alone justifies us, and not works.' The matter itself, and not the nature of the language only, compels this translation...Paul's words are too strong; they endure no works, none at all; and if it is not a work, it must be by faith alone. How could it be such a fine, improving inoffensive doctrine, if people were taught that they might become righteous by works, beside faith? That would be as much as to say that it was not Christ's death alone that takes away our sins, but that our works, too, did something toward it; and it would be a fine honoring of Christ's death to say that our works helped it and could do that which He does, and that we were good and strong like Him. This is of the devil, who cannot leave the blood of Christ without abuse![111]

Trust in Christ as Savior is a key element of saving faith. But this faith is more than an intellectual assent to truth. Faith *is* based on the knowledge God has given us of his truth in Christ. There must be an assent to that knowledge, that is, an implicit acceptance of the truth. However, truth must then become personalized in a relationship with Christ. A response of personal trust in and commitment to Christ is called for in scripture. Faith involves the whole man: the mind, emotions and will. It means entering into a personal relationship with Christ through an act of personal commitment to him. It involves the receiving of Christ as well as the giving of oneself to him.

To limit the definition of faith, as some do—to believing and accepting truth only—is to undermine its biblical meaning. Salvation must be appropriated and that is done by appropriating the person of Christ. Scripture states that we must *receive* Christ: 'But as many as received Him, to them He gave the power to become the children of God, even to those who believe in His name...As you therefore have *received* Christ Jesus as Lord, so walk in Him' (Jn. 1:12; Col. 2:6). We cannot appropriate a particular aspect of Christ's work independent of Christ himself. We are to receive *Christ* the person as our Lord and Savior. In receiving him we receive salvation. It is not only our belief in the doctrine of justification that saves us but the receiving of Christ. It is Christ who justifies, Christ who saves. And out of our union with him we receive the benefits of salvation. As John Gerstner puts it:

> Eternal life depends on Christ alone—nothing, but nothing else. Predestination will not bring it. Providence cannot produce it. It does not rest on foreknowledge, divine decrees, or even the atonement itself. *Eternal life is Christ dwelling in His righteousness in the soul of the justified person.* So eternal life is union with Jesus Christ. And the word for that union with Jesus Christ is faith...Strictly speaking, the true Christian church does not teach justification by faith. It teaches justification by Christ. Where does faith come in? It is simply the uniting with, joining with, becoming one with, the Lord Jesus Christ.[112]

That faith means the *appropriation* of the person of Christ is expounded by the following theologians:

> **John Calvin:** Faith of itself does not possess the power of justifying, but only in so far as it receives Christ...From this it is to be inferred that, in teaching that before his righteousness is received Christ is received in faith, we do not take the power of justifying away from Christ[113]...Christ was given to us by God's generosity, to be grasped and possessed by us in faith. By partaking of him, we principally receive a double grace[114]...Faith embraces Christ, as offered to us by the Father.[115]

John Flavel: Christ and his benefits go inseparably and undividedly together: it is Christ himself who is made all this (wisdom, righteousness, sanctification, redemption) unto us: we can have no saving benefit separate and apart from the person of Christ: many would willingly receive his privileges, who will not receive his person; but it cannot be; if we will have one, we must take the other too: Yea, we must accept his person first, and then his benefits.[116]

A.A. Hodge: The Scriptures make it plain that the condition of its effectual application (redemption) is an act of faith, involving real spiritual repentance and the turning from sin and the acceptance and self–appropriation of Christ and his redemption as the only remedy.[117]

Louis Berkhof: Finally there are also the figures of coming to Christ and receiving Him, John 5:40; 7:37 (cf. vs. 38); 6:44,65; 1:12. The figure of coming to Christ pictures faith as an action in which man looks away from himself and his own merits, to be clothed with the righteousness of Jesus Christ; and that of receiving Christ stresses the fact that faith is an appropriating organ[118]...Faith is the instrument by which we appropriate Christ and His righteousness[119]...Faith justifies in so far as it takes possession of Christ.[120]...Faith is not merely a matter of the intellect, nor of the intellect and the emotions combined; it is also a matter of the will, determining the direction of the soul, an act of the soul going out towards its object and appropriating this. Without this activity the object of faith, which the sinner recognizes as true and real and entirely applicable to his present needs, remains outside of him. And in saving faith it is a matter of life and death that the object be appropriated.[121]

The Westminster Confession of Faith: The principal acts of saving faith are, accepting, receiving, and resting upon Christ alone for justification, sanctification and eternal life, by virtue of the covenant of grace.[122]

These comments have direct bearing on the ongoing debate over the nature of saving faith and lordship salvation within evangelicalism today. Since salvation is experienced through being rightly related to the person of Christ and since Christ is Lord as well as Savior, then an important aspect of saving faith will be commitment to Christ as Lord since he cannot be divided in his person. There are some who suggest that lordship salvation is a perversion of the teaching of the Reformation. Nothing could be further from the truth. The Reformers consistently defined saving faith as the *receiving* of Christ (the whole person) in all of his offices as Prophet, Priest and King. They speak of his indwelling the human heart. They teach that this saving relationship cannot be separated from repentance and sanctification of the heart. Unless the individual submits his heart to Christ as Lord, the heart is not sanctified. Saving faith, therefore, involves not only trust in Christ but commitment and submission of life to him as well. He cannot be received as Priest (Savior), and not be received as King (Lord) and Prophet. His person cannot be divided. John Flavel says this:

> The very essence of saving faith consists in our receiving Christ...Christ is offered us in the gospel entirely and undividedly, as clothed with all his offices, priestly, prophetical, and regal; as Christ Jesus the Lord, Acts xv.31, and so the true believer receives him;...As without any of these offices, the work of our salvation could not be completed, so without acceptance of Christ in them all, our union with him by faith cannot be completed...The gospel offer of Christ includes all his offices, and gospel–faith just so receives him; to submit to him, as well as to be redeemed by him; to imitate him in the holiness of life, as well as to reap the purchases and fruits of his death. It must be an entire receiving of the Lord Jesus Christ...See that you receive all Christ, with all your heart. To receive all Christ is to receive his person, clothed with all his offices; and to receive him with all your heart, is to receive him into your understanding, will

and affections, Acts viii.37. As there is nothing in Christ that may be refused, so there is nothing in you from which he must be excluded.[123]

So, although saving faith will include knowledge of and assent to the facts of the gospel and trust in Christ as Savior it also means a commitment of the life to him as Lord. Berkhof, for example, states: 'Faith...consists in a personal trust in Christ as Savior and Lord, including the surrender of the soul...to Christ, and a recognition and appropriation of Christ as the source of pardon and of spiritual life.'[124] He speaks here of a surrender of the soul to Christ as Lord. Calvin teaches that obedience is inherent in the nature of saving faith:

> That very assent itself—as I have already partially suggested, and will reiterate more fully—is more of the heart than of the brain, and more of the disposition than of the understanding. For this reason it is called 'obedience of faith' (Rom. 1:5), and the Lord prefers no other obedience to it—and justly, since nothing is more precious to him than this truth...But another much clearer argument now offers itself. Since faith embraces Christ, as offered to us by the Father (cf. John 6:29)—that is, since he is offered not only for righteousness, forgiveness of sins, and peace, but also for sanctification (cf. 1 Cor. 1:30) and the fountain of the water of life (John 7:38; cf. ch. 4:14)—without a doubt, no one can truly know him without at the same time apprehending the sanctification of the Spirit. Or, if anyone desires some plainer statement, faith rests upon the knowledge of Christ. And Christ cannot be known apart from the sanctification of his Spirit. It follows that faith can in no wise be separated from a devout disposition.[125]

A.A. Hodge makes it clear that saving faith is not only trust in Christ as Savior but submission of the life to him as Lord:

> The Scriptures make it plain that the condition of its effectual

application (redemption) is an act of faith, involving real spiritual repentance and the turning from sin and the acceptance and self-appropriation of Christ and of His redemption as the only remedy...From within, the God–man reigns supreme in every Christian heart. It is impossible to accept Christ as our Sacrifice and Priest without at the same time cordially accepting him as our Prophet, absolutely submitting our understanding to his teaching, and accepting him as our King, submitting implicitly our hearts and wills and lives to his sovereign control. Paul delights to call himself the *doulos*, purchased servant, of Jesus Christ. Every Christian spontaneously calls him our *Lord* Jesus. His will is our law, his love our motive, his glory our end. To obey his will, to work in his service, to fight his battles, to triumph in his victories, is our whole life and joy.[126]

In his book, *Faith Alone*, R.C. Sproul documents the teaching of the seventeenth century Reformed theologians, Herman Witsius and Francis Turretin. He points out that their concept of saving faith includes knowledge, assent and trust, and commitment to Christ as Lord:

Of this aspect (act of reception and union) Turretin declares that it is the act 'by which we not only seek Christ through a desire of the soul and fly to him, but apprehend and receive him offered, embrace him found, apply him to ourselves and adhere to and unite ourselves to him.' Witsius calls this the *formal and principal* act of faith. By this act of faith the believer becomes united with Christ. This act is what the New Testament speaks of as 'receiving' Christ. Witsius says: 'By this act, Christ becomes, so to speak, the peculiar property of the believing soul. All that belongs to Christ being exhibited together with him, the believer claims to himself whatever is Christ's, and especially his righteousness, which is the foundation of salvation.'

Witsius says of surrender: '...when the believer thus receives Christ and rests upon him, he considers him not merely as SAVIOR, but also as LORD. He receives a whole Christ, and acquiesces in him in all those characters which he sustains: but he is not less a Lord than a Savior; nay, he cannot be a Savior, unless he be also a Lord.'[127]

Sproul goes on to say that while the Reformed understanding of faith is usually defined by the three main categories of knowledge (*notitia*), assent (*assensus*) and trust (*fiducia*), these do not negate commitment to Christ as Lord. He says that commitment to Christ's Lordship comes under the heading of trust or *fiducia*. In other words, it is an essential part of what it means to trust in Christ. As Sproul puts it: 'These further elaborations of aspects of faith, whose number varies among Reformed theologians like Turretin and Witsius, may also be subsumed under the heading of *fiducia*.'[128]

John Murray makes the point that inherent in the nature of faith is a renunciation of sin. He says it is exercised in conjunction with repentance. Thus, the essence of faith is *commitment* to Christ:

> Justification is by faith and therefore can never be separated from it. What is this faith? It is trust in Christ for salvation from sin. It is to contradict the very nature of faith to regard it as anything else than a sin–hating, sin–condemning, and sin–renouncing principle. Since faith is a whole–souled movement of trust in Christ its very spring and motive is salvation from sin...As regeneration is the fountain of faith and faith is the logical pre–condition of justification, we can never think of justification apart from regeneration. And, again, the faith that justifies is faith conjoined with repentance.[129]...Faith is in its essence commitment to Christ that we may be saved. The premise of that commitment is that we are unsaved and we believe on Christ in order that we may be saved...It is to lost sinners that Christ is offered, and the demand of that overture is simply and solely that we commit ourselves to him in order that we may be saved.[130]

R.L. Dabney issues this warning:

> Faith embraces Christ substantially in all His offices. This
> must be urged as of prime practical importance...Our
> Catechism defines faith, as embracing Christ 'as He is offered
> in the gospel.' Our Confession (chap. xiv.2) says: 'the
> principal acts of saving faith are accepting, receiving, and
> resting upon Christ alone for justification, sanctification and
> eternal life.' How Christ is offered us in the gospel, may be
> seen in Matt. 1:21; 1 Cor. 1:30; Eph. 5:25-27; Titus 1:14. The
> tendency of human selfishness is ever to degrade Christ's
> sacrifice into a mere expedient for bestowing impunity. The
> pastor can never be too explicit in teaching that this is a
> travesty of the gospel; and that no one rises above the faith of
> the stony–ground hearer, until he desires and embraces
> Christ as deliverer from the depravity of sin, as well as hell.[131]

Thomas Watson says:

> How shall I know that I am making a right application of
> Christ? A hypocrite may think he applies when he does not.
> Balaam, though a sorcerer, still said, 'my God' (*Numb.
> 22:18*). Answer: He who rightly applies Christ puts these two
> together, Jesus and Lord: 'Christ Jesus my Lord' (*Phil. 3:8*).
> Many take Christ as Jesus, but refuse him as Lord. Do you
> join 'Prince and Saviour' (*Acts 5:31*)? Would you as well be
> ruled by Christ's laws as saved by his blood? Christ is 'a priest
> upon his throne' (*Zech. 6:13*). He will never be a priest to
> intercede unless your heart is the throne where he sways his
> sceptre. A true applying of Christ is when we take him as a
> husband that we give ourselves to him as Lord.[132]

These comments make it clear that saving faith involves more
than trusting in Christ for imputed righteousness and
forgiveness of sin only. As we have seen, the call of God to
sinful man is a call to faith and repentance. The biblical
teaching of faith alone (*sola fide*) is always put in contrast to

works in scripture. But it is never placed in opposition to repentance. Faith alone means Christ alone by grace alone. But the faith that saves is always accompanied by evangelical repentance.

This underscores again the crucial importance of a *relationship* with Christ. Salvation is knowing a person, the Lord Jesus Christ. As Jesus himself said: 'This is life eternal, that they may know Thee, the only true God, and Jesus Christ whom Thou hast sent' (Jn. 17:3). All doctrine is to lead us to and leave us with the person of God.

There is a potential danger which needs to be addressed here. The Protestant Reformers stressed the biblical teaching of the grace of God in salvation. Historically this teaching has come to be known as the Doctrines of Grace. The inherent danger here is that of defining Christianity by a system of doctrine to the neglect of the centerpiece of true Christianity: a *relationship* with the person of Christ. We must be careful that a system of doctrine does not become an end in itself and displace the relationship. Our focus must be on the person of Christ, not on the Doctrines of Grace. This danger is subtle but can be deadly. We can know doctrine and not know Christ. We can be completely orthodox doctrinally and yet have a dead faith. We can end up with another form of scholasticism, dressed in Reformed clothing. Doctrine is both foundational and essential to faith, but it is not the essence of it. The heart of Christianity is Christ. We cannot separate a true relationship with Christ from doctrine because doctrine forms the foundation of knowledge necessary for entering that relationship. Unfortunately, though, it is possible to separate doctrine from the relationship resulting in dead orthodoxy.

Let me illustrate. As mentioned in the chapter on justification, a commonly used term for the imputed righteousness of Christ is 'an alien righteousness.' This means that the righteousness that justifies is a righteousness that is achieved completely outside of us and is not to be confused with regeneration or sanctification. Out of genuine concern for safeguarding this truth some have fallen into error regarding it. For example, I was told by a member of a Reformed Church recently that salvation has nothing to do with the consecration of the believer or with the work of Christ inside the believer but only with faith in the alien righteousness of Christ imputed to the believer. He does not believe that it is the indwelling Christ that gives us favor and acceptance with God. His focus on salvation is totally and exclusively on justification and imputed righteousness. But this is a repudiation of the Reformation teaching. John Calvin himself insists on the absolute necessity for the indwelling Christ for salvation:

> I confess that we are deprived of this utterly incomparable good until Christ is made ours. Therefore, that joining together of Head and members, *that indwelling of Christ in our hearts*—in short, that mystical union—are accorded by us the highest degree of importance, so that Christ, having been made ours, makes us sharers with him in the gifts with which he has been endowed. We do not, therefore, contemplate him outside ourselves from afar in order that his righteousness may be imputed to us but because we put on Christ and are grafted into his body—in short, because he deigns to make us one with him. For this reason, we glory that we have fellowship of righteousness with him (emphasis mine).[133]

Imputed righteousness is a glorious truth but to preach it to the exclusion of the other aspects of salvation is wrong and dangerous. Men are exhorted to look outside of themselves to Christ for the righteousness they need to stand before God. However, though the righteousness that saves is external to the individual who receives Christ, Christ himself is *not*. We do not receive righteousness apart from receiving the person of Christ himself. The Reformers stressed the importance of the indwelling Christ relative to justification. They taught that an elemental aspect of saving faith is the *appropriation* of Christ as a person and it is his *indwelling* that secures salvation for us. Martyn Lloyd–Jones makes these perceptive and penetrating observations about the dangers of knowledge and doctrine divorced from this vital relationship with Christ:

> There is no need, of course, to emphasize the fact that knowledge is all–important. We can never know too much. Knowledge is essential, doctrine is vital. The Bible is full of doctrine, and the New Testament particularly so. The epistles are mighty, glorious expositions of doctrine and of truth...Knowledge, therefore, is in and of itself absolutely essential; indeed we must give it priority, and see to it that it always comes first...But, it is possible for us to develop a false notion of knowledge...to take a purely theoretical and academic interest in truth and knowledge, to make knowledge an end in itself—the purely theoretical and academic approach...This danger is one of knowing 'about' a subject rather than knowing it. 'Knowing about!' What a vital distinction this is. What a difference there is between preaching about the gospel and preaching the gospel! It is possible to preach round the gospel and say things about it without ever presenting it. That is quite useless—indeed it can be very dangerous. It may be true of us that we know 'about' these things, but do not really know them. And this, of course, becomes all–important when we realize that the whole end and object of theology is to know God! A Person! Not a collection of abstract truths, not a number of philosophical propositions, but God! a Person! To know Him!—'the only true God, and Jesus Christ, whom thou hast sent!'

> If you just go in for that sort of theoretical intellectual knowledge, the devil will let you talk of doctrine enough; you will turn from Arminianism to Calvinism, you shall be orthodox enough, if you will be content to live without Christ's living in you. The devil does not care at all whether you change from being an Arminian to being a Calvinist if you do not know Christ and if you do not know God. One is as bad as the other. A theoretical Calvinism is of no more value than

a theoretical Arminianism—not the slightest...Doctrine after all is a foundation, and no more. It is not an end, it is only a beginning. It is the means. We must never stop at it. It is always designed to bring us, by faith, into that knowledge, that intimacy, that deep experience of the Living God, in which we really meet with Him, know that He is present, and are conscious of the energies of the Spirit in us and amongst us...And if it does not do that we shall merely have been turning round in circles, giving a good deal of satisfaction to the flesh. We shall go away proud of our knowledge and our understanding, but it will be of no help to anybody at all.[134]

Conversion

We must have both a doctrinal and an experiential knowledge of Christ. This is just another way of saying there must be true conversion. Conversion is the theological term that describes the human role of appropriation and commitment in salvation. We are commanded in scripture to convert to Christ. Matthew 18:3 states: 'Truly, truly, I say to you, unless you are *converted* and become like children, you shall not enter the kingdom of heaven.' Peter says: 'Repent ye therefore, and *be converted*, that your sins may be blotted out' (Acts 3:19). It is a part of the gospel call to sinful men and the evidence of regeneration. As John Murray states:

The response to the call is a whole–souled movement of loving subjection and trust in God. It is a totality act of man's soul...It is a turning to God with the whole heart and soul and strength and mind...This change of heart manifests itself in faith and repentance, which are the responses of our whole inner man to the revelation of the gospel, away from sin and towards God.[135]

Repentance and faith are defined by the word *turn*. We are commanded in scripture to turn from sin to God in Christ to be saved. Turning to God is, as Murray puts it: 'a whole–

souled movement of loving subjection and trust in God.' In 1 Thessalonians 1:9 Paul describes the conversion experience of those at Thessalonica: 'And how you turned *to* God *from* idols to *serve* the living and true God.' The Reformers stressed the necessity for conversion. This is also the consistent teaching of those theologians who have remained true to the heritage of the Reformation. Berkhof states:

> The most common (Old Testament) word for conversion, means to turn, to turn about, and to return...The word clearly shows that, what the Old Testament calls conversion, is a return to Him from whom sin has separated man...True conversion is born of godly sorrow, and issues in a life of devotion to God, II Cor. 7:10...Conversion marks the conscious beginning, not only of the putting away of the old man, a fleeing from sin, but also of the putting on of the new man, a striving for holiness of life. In regeneration the sinful principle of the old life is already replaced by the holy principle of the new life. But it is only in conversion that this transition penetrates into the conscious life, turning it into a new and Godward direction. The sinner consciously forsakes the old sinful life and turns to a life in communion with and devoted to God...(Conversion is) a conscious turning from sin unto God...In the case of adults...conversion is absolutely essential (for salvation)...Conversion is necessary in the case of adults in the sense that its elements, namely, repentance and faith must be present in their lives.
>
> If we take the word conversion in its most specific sense, it denotes a change that takes place once and cannot be repeated...Conversion consists in repentance and faith, so that faith is really a part of conversion...There is no doubt that, logically, repentance and the knowledge of sin precedes the faith that yields to Christ in trusting love.[136]

This truth is also seen in the words of Christ to the apostle Paul when he describes the nature of the gospel ministry to which he was being called:

And I said, 'Who art Thou, Lord?' And the Lord said, 'I am Jesus whom you are persecuting. 'But arise, and stand on your feet; for this purpose I have appeared to you, to appoint you a minister and a witness not only to the things which you have seen, but also to the things in which I will appear to you; delivering you from the Jewish people and from the Gentiles, to whom I am sending you, to open their eyes so that they may turn from darkness to light and from the dominion of Satan to God, in order that they may receive forgiveness of sins and an inheritance among those who have been sanctified by faith in Me' (Acts 26:15–18).

Jesus stressed the necessity for conversion. As we have seen, man apart from Christ in his unregenerate state, is under the authority and power of Satan. Part of Christ's work in salvation is to deliver us from this state. In Acts 26, Jesus describes how this takes place. The apostle Paul is commissioned to preach the gospel—to bring men truth—to open their eyes. The objective of this spiritual enlightenment is that they might be saved; turned from darkness to light, from the dominion of Satan to God in order that they might receive forgiveness of sins and an inheritance among those who are sanctified through faith in Christ. Here is beautifully pictured for us the process of conversion, the negative and positive aspects of salvation—the turning from sin to Christ, from darkness to light (from sin to righteousness)and from the dominion of Satan to (the dominion of) God. Men are called upon to renounce the authority and dominion of Satan in their lives by submitting themselves to the authority or dominion of God. Authority is the ultimate issue.

Conversion is the work of regeneration and definitive sanctification whereby one enters the kingdom of God through saving faith. It results in a radical change in the heart, nature, life purpose and direction of an individual. Prior to conversion there was a preoccupation with and the promotion of selfish interests. The new convert is now submitted to God, filled with love for him, pursues holiness and the promotion of the kingdom of God. Paul sums it up when he says: 'He died for all, that they who live should no longer live for themselves, but for Him who died and rose again on their behalf' (2 Cor. 5:15). Christ's purpose in salvation is to effect not only our forgiveness but to bring us into a relationship with God that we might fulfil his purpose for us: glorifying him, loving him, trusting him and living for him.

Scripture teaches that conversion is a thing of the heart. The question is not how orthodox are our beliefs, how much biblical knowledge we possess, or how active we are in ministry, but are we a new creation—a servant of God? The proof of our profession is in how we live. The ultimate test of true Christianity is a changed and sanctified life. As the apostle John put it: 'The one who says he abides in Him ought himself to walk in the same manner as He walked' (1 Jn. 2:6). Only a new nature and a changed life are adequate proofs of the presence of God's saving grace. Jonathan Edwards points out the danger of having a sound knowledge of the Christian faith without true conversion:

> In a *legal humiliation* men are made sensible that they are nothing before the great and terrible God, and that they are undone, and wholly insufficient to help themselves....but they have not an *answerable frame* of heart, consisting in a disposition to abase themselves, and exalt God alone. This disposition is given only in *evangelical* humiliation, by overcoming the heart, and changing its inclination....In a legal humiliation the conscience is convinced....but because there is no spiritual understanding, the will is not bowed, nor the inclination altered....In legal humiliation, men are brought to despair of helping themselves; in evangelical, they are brought voluntarily to deny and renounce themselves: in the former they are subdued and brought to the ground; in the latter, they are brought sweetly to yield, and freely and with delight to prostrate themselves at the feet of God.
>
> Men may be legally humbled and have no humility....they may be thoroughly convinced that they have no righteousness, but are altogether sinful, exceedingly guilty, and justly exposed to eternal damnation—and be fully sensible of their

own helplessness—without the least mortification of the pride of their hearts...But the essence of evangelical humiliation consists in a mean esteem of himself, as in himself nothing, and altogether contemptible and odious....and....in denying his natural self–exaltation, and renouncing his own dignity and glory, and in being emptied of himself; so that he does freely, and from his very heart, as it were renounce, and annihilate himself. Thus the Christian doth in evangelical humiliation....This is a great and most essential thing in true religion. The whole frame of the gospel, every thing appertaining to the new covenant and all God's dispensations towards fallen men, are calculated to bring to pass this effect. They that are destitute of this, have no true religion, whatever profession they may make, and how high soever their religious affections....God has abundantly manifested in his word, that this is what he has a peculiar respect to in his saints and that nothing is acceptable to him without it....As we would therefore make the Holy Scriptures our rule, in judging of....our own religious qualifications and state; it concerns us greatly to look at this humiliation, as one of the most essential things pertaining to true Christianity.[137]

Application

In light of the need for conversion there are a number of important points which need to be emphasized. God is absolutely sovereign in the work of salvation. It is he who accomplishes the work and applies it to man. From beginning to end it is a gift received from God. However, when presenting this truth we must be careful not to minimize human responsibility. Repentance and faith are the human responses demanded by God to the proclamation of his gospel. They are both gifts of God but also the activities of man. In the appropriation of salvation men are not passive. John Murray emphasizes that repentance and faith are duties to be pressed upon men with great earnestness:

Faith is not regeneration, for it is the person who believes.

But it is by the washing and renewal of regeneration that the person is enabled to believe. Faith is of God, but faith itself is the whole–souled movement of the person in entrustment to Christ...It is at this point of faith that our responsibility enters...It is truly our responsibility to be what regeneration effects, namely, new creatures, trusting, loving, and obeying God with all our heart and soul and mind...Faith is the activity of the person and him alone. And every Godward response is, of course, our responsibility. *This needs to be pressed home with the utmost emphasis.*[138]

Obviously, then, this has important implications for the preaching of the gospel. In conversion, a man turns wholly from sin to God. He is very active in this process even though it is a gift of God from start to finish. This is a mystery, but we must beware lest we so exalt the truth of the sovereignty of God that we denigrate the scriptural emphasis on the responsibility of man. B.B. Warfield expresses it this way:

As it is the single duty laid by the Ascended Christ on His messengers that they shall open men's eyes, the single duty He lays on their hearers is correspondingly that they should turn from the darkness to the light, and (what is the same thing) from the power of Satan to God. It is, of course, as evident that men cannot turn from darkness to light, from the tyranny of Satan to God, in their own strength, as it is that men cannot open other people's eyes by their own power. As in the one case, so in the other, the immanent work of the Holy Spirit is not excluded because it is not mentioned. But as in the one case, so in the other, the action of man is required. Christ requires His apostle to 'open men's eyes'—that is, to proclaim the truth which opens their eyes. Christ requires their hearers to turn from darkness to light, to shake off their bondage to Satan and to turn to God. In both cases, He requires the 'sowing' and 'watering,' while it is He alone who gives the increase.[139]

We must not back away from the strong demands of the scriptures and the teaching of Christ. We must preach to men about sin and about Christ (his person and work). We are to impress upon them their solemn responsibility to respond— to come to Christ in true repentance and faith. In this we are to rely solely upon our sovereign God to enable them to do so. But we must hold before men the truth—salvation means receiving the person of Christ as Lord and Savior. If we fail to do this we have failed to present the biblical gospel to lost men. As J.I. Packer has commented:

> In the last analysis there is only one method of evangelism, namely the faithful explanation and application of the gospel message...We have to ask: is the way we present the gospel calculated to convey to people the application of the gospel and not just part of it, but the whole of it—the summons to see and know oneself as God sees and knows one, that is as a sinful creature and to face the breadth and depth of the need into which a wrong relationship with God has brought one, and to face too the cost and consequences of turning to receive Christ as Savior and Lord? Or is it likely to be deficient here and to gloss over some of this, and to give an inadequate distorted impression of what the gospel requires?...Will it leave people supposing that all they have to do is to trust Christ as sin–bearer not realizing that they must also deny themselves and enthrone Him as their Lord (the error which we might call only–believisim)?[140]

Divine sovereignty, regeneration, union with Christ, the finished work of the atonement, justification by imputed righteousness, sanctification, adoption, repentance, faith (as trust in and commitment to Christ as Lord and Savior), conversion—salvation by grace alone through faith alone on account of Christ alone—these are the essentials of the Reformation gospel. It is this teaching which we find confirmed by Jesus himself.

~ 11 ~

Salvation According to Jesus

*Come to Me, all who are weary and heavy–laden, and I will
give you rest. Take My yoke upon you and learn from Me, for
I am gentle and humble in heart; and you shall find rest for
your souls. For My yoke is easy and My load is light (Matthew
11:28–30)*

When teaching on salvation Jesus has a great deal to say
about hell, the kingdom of God, his atonement, union
with himself, conversion, faith, repentance, sanctification and
discipleship. Surprisingly, he has little to say about
justification. In the context of Protestant–Roman Catholic
ecumenism, Harold O.J. Brown recently made an interesting
observation about the teaching of Christ. Referring to liberal
Protestants and Catholics he states:

> It is true that they have reduced the old hostility between the
> confessions, but unfortunately, in order to hold them, as both
> of these groups...do, one has to ignore some of the most
> explicit teachings of Jesus Himself.[141]

These comments apply to our present study. In order to hold
our personal or denominational views on salvation, do we
ignore or reinterpret some of the teachings of Jesus?

In any study of Jesus' teaching on salvation what is striking
is his constant focus upon himself as the source of salvation.
'Come to me, follow me, believe in me, drink of me' (Mt.
11:28–30; Mk. 8:34–38; Jn. 6:35; Jn. 7:38) are his constant

cries. He says, 'I am the way the truth and the life; no one comes to the Father, but through Me' (Jn. 14:6). According to Jesus, it is through a personal relationship with him that one comes into the experience of salvation.

He preaches the absolute necessity for the new birth (Jn. 3:3–6), for conversion (Mt. 18:3) and for sanctification (Mt. 7:21–24). He tells men that it is only those who do the will of God who will enter the kingdom of heaven, that those who truly belong to him will manifest the reality of that relationship by bearing the fruit of obedience in their lives (Jn. 15:1–8; 8:31).

He says that none can come to him except the Father first draw them (Jn. 6:44) and yet he calls men to repentance and faith (Mk. 1:15; Jn. 3:16; Lk. 13:3; Jn. 4:15–18).

He teaches that justification is not by works but based solely on the mercy of God (Lk. 18:9–14). He emphasizes faith in himself and his atoning work as the sole basis for salvation and complete deliverance from judgment and condemnation (Jn. 3:14–16; 6:35, 47–58, 5:24, 10:27–29), but he also equally emphasizes his authority as Lord, as clearly seen in his call to discipleship. His teaching on discipleship is his definitive teaching on the kingdom of God and what it means to enter into a relationship with himself. There is perhaps no greater confusion within evangelicalism in our day, however, than that which relates to this subject. For this reason we will look at it in some detail.

Christ's Call to Discipleship

In Luke 14, Jesus gives the following conditions of discipleship:

> If anyone comes to Me and does not hate his own father and mother and wife and children and brothers and sisters, yes, and even his own life, he cannot be my disciple (Lk. 14:26).
>
> Whoever does not carry his own cross and come after Me cannot be My disciple (Lk. 14:27).

So therefore no one of you can be My disciple who does not give up all his own possessions (Lk. 14:33).

Jesus is not talking here about a process but a *commitment* to him to become a disciple. A biblical commitment to Christ will result in a process of growth, but in this particular passage Christ is not talking about the process. He is referring to the initial commitment to himself. Let us examine his words to see exactly what he means.

Luke 14:26: 'If anyone comes to Me and does not hate his own father and mother and wife and children and brothers and sisters, yes, and even his own life, he cannot be My disciple.'

To interpret Jesus' meaning accurately, especially the word hate, we need to refer to Matthew 10:37: 'He who loves father or mother more than Me is not worthy of Me; he who loves son or daughter more than Me is not worthy of Me.'

Jesus is dealing here with love and devotion. He demands first place in our hearts. He must be preeminent in the life— our First Love. All other relationships are to take a secondary place in relation to himself. William Hendriksen makes the following comments on this verse:

He tells the people that devotion to Himself must be so wholehearted that even attachment to parents and to other members of one's family must not be allowed to stand in the way. Clearly the meaning of the word hate in the Lucan passage is to love less. In all things Christ must always have the pre–eminence (Col 1:18).That the word hate in Luke 14:26 cannot have the meaning which we generally attach to it is clear also from the fact that Jesus tells us to love even our enemies (Matt 5:44).

What the Savior demands in Luke 14:26 and other passages is complete devotion, the type of loyalty that is so true and unswerving that every other attachment, even to one's own life must be subjected to it. If a person is unwilling to tender that unconditional devotion, then says Jesus, 'he cannot be

My disciple.'[142]

Luke 14:27: 'Anyone who does not carry his own cross and come after Me cannot be My disciple.'

The issue here is one of self denial. We will be looking at this more thoroughly later, but these words by Campbell Morgan capsualize the Lord's meaning:

> What is self denial?. . .To deny self is to say no to every wish that comes out of the personal life. To deny self is radical. It goes down to the roots of things. A man may practice self denial all his life and never deny himself. A man may practice self denial in this and that respect, and all the while his self-centeredness is strengthened. Jesus did not say exercise self denial in externalities. He said deny self, have done with choosing, wishing, planning, arranging for self. Choose no more, will no more, except to will that God shall will...I deny self when I hand over the keys of the citadel to the king and say, Enter and reign in every chamber of the being, in all possibilities of the soul.[143]

Jesus must be first in my affections, and his will must come first in my life. My will must be submitted to his will. He must be Lord.

Luke 14:33: 'So therefore, no one of you can be My disciple who does not give up all his own possessions.'

William Hendriksen states, 'Wholehearted devotion, all–out loyalty, complete self denial, so that one places himself, his time, his earthly possessions, his talents etc., at the disposal of Christ, is what Jesus asks.'[144]

In summation, then, Jesus calls for the unconditional surrender of self to him as Lord and First Love in order to become his disciple. These are the conditions he sets forth for entering into a relationship with himself. And the point Jesus is making is that apart from this commitment there is no salvation.

To demonstrate that this interpretation of Luke 14 is

accurate it is necessary that we look carefully at a number of other passages on discipleship: Mark 8:34–37, John 12:24–26, Matthew 11:28–30 and Mark 10:17–22. There are three general word pictures used by Jesus in these passages to illustrate his teaching on salvation and discipleship: the cross, the yoke and the grain of wheat. They each describe the attitude towards self we must adopt if we are to be rightly related to him.

Mark 8:34–37: The Cross

> And He summoned the multitude with His disciples, and said to them, 'If anyone wishes to come after Me, let him deny himself, and take up his cross, and follow Me. For whoever wishes to save his life shall lose it; but whoever loses his life for My sake and the gospel's shall save it. For what does it profit a man to gain the whole world, and forfeit his soul? For what shall a man give in exchange for his soul?' (Cf. Lk. 9:23–27).

This passage is foundational to discipleship. Mark 8:34 is in principle the same verse as Luke 14:27. But here in Mark 8 Jesus goes into a deeper explanation of the meaning of discipleship.

These words of Jesus follow Peter's attempt to dissuade the Lord from the path of the cross. Peter is met with a stern, severe rebuke from Jesus. His reply is instructive because it reveals to us the master principle that governed his life, and it forms the backdrop to his additional comments to the disciples and the multitude. Jesus rejects Peter's suggestion, ascribing it to Satan, and says to him: 'You are not setting your mind on God's interests, but man's' (Mk. 8:33). Jesus sets forth a contrast between two life principles: God's interests and man's interests. The two are in conflict with one another. Jesus was controlled by one master passion: To know and do the will of his Father no matter what the cost. Jesus' life was not governed by his own interests, but those of his Father's.

He stated over and over again: 'I have come down from heaven, not to do My own will, but the will of Him who sent Me' (Jn. 6:38). Thus, self interest is the antithesis of the life of Christ. His passion was the will of God, for the glory of God, even if it meant persecution, suffering and death on a cross!

This stark contrast between man's interests and God's interests forms the context in which Jesus teaches about the cross and what it means to follow him. Being a follower of Jesus means adopting the same attitude towards my life that he had towards his. Jesus says that if any man would come after him he must do three things: deny himself, take up his cross, and follow him. What does he mean?

Deny self—This means a turning from self–will, renouncing living for self. John Stott says: 'Self denied...is not to deny things to myself, but to deny myself to myself. It is to say no to self and yes to Christ; to repudiate self and acknowledge Christ.'[145]

Take up the cross—a cross is an instrument of death and is used in a metaphorical sense by Jesus. When it is used in conjunction with the phrase 'deny self', it carries the idea of dying to my right to myself, my own interests and ambitions. John Stott comments: 'To take up a cross is to put oneself into the position of a condemned man on his way to execution. In other words, the attitude to self is that of crucifixion. Everyday the Christian is to die. Everyday he renounces the sovereignty to his own will. Everyday he renews his unconditional surrender to Jesus Christ.'[146]

Follow me—The tense of this verb indicates the meaning is to follow continually. Thayer's *Greek English Lexicon of the New Testament* defines the Greek word follow to mean 'to join one as a disciple, to become or be his disciple.' To follow Jesus therefore means that in becoming a disciple I must first die to myself in order to live for him.

Why the imperative call to deny self, take up a cross and follow Jesus? *'For'*, he says, 'whosoever will save his life shall *lose* it, but whosoever shall lose his life for my sake and the gospel's the same shall save it' (Mk. 8:35). The key to understanding this verse is the word *lose*. 'Lose' is the same Greek word that is translated *perish* in other parts of the New Testament. It means to die eternally:

> (The Lord) is not willing that any should *perish*, but that all should come to repentance (2 Pet. 3:9).
>
> For God so loved the world, that he gave his only begotten Son, that whoever believes in Him should not *perish*, but have eternal life (Jn. 3:16).

To insure that we fully understand these issues Jesus further explains and emphasizes his point in verses 36–37:

> For what shall it profit a man, if he shall gain the whole world and lose his own soul? Or what shall a man give in exchange for his soul?

Jesus says that if a man does not deny self, take up a cross and commit to be his follower or disciple then that man will *perish*—he will forfeit his soul. Jesus makes this same point in John 10:27–28 when he again uses the word 'follow' to describe *his* sheep:

> My sheep hear My voice, and I know them, and they *follow* Me; and I give eternal life to them, and they shall never perish; and no one shall snatch them out of My hand.

Who are the true sheep of the Lord Jesus? Who are the ones who hear his voice, to whom he gives eternal life and who will therefore never perish? It is those who *follow* him; those who commit themselves to him as disciples. The issue is one of eternity and salvation. R.C.H. Lenski and William Hendriksen make this clear in their comments on Mark 8:34:

> **Lenski**: This is not self denial in the current sense of the word but *true conversion*, the very first essential of the Christian life.[147]

> **Hendriksen**: Together the three (deny self, take up a cross, and follow me) indicate true conversion followed by a life long sanctification.[148]

In Mark 8 and Luke 14 Jesus is setting forth conditions for entering the kingdom of God. When he uses the term disciple, he uses it as a synonym for the term Christian. To become a disciple is to become a Christian. To become a Christian is to become a disciple. William Hendriksen's comments on the demands of Christ in Mark 8:34 and Luke 9:23 are worth noting:

> In the next three verses...the obligation to be converted, etc., and the reward that results are brought into sharp contrast with the loss experienced by those who refuse to deny themselves, to take up their cross, and to follow Jesus...Accordingly, with an implied 'Let him not refuse,' there follows...For whoever would save his life shall lose it, but whoever loses his life for my sake, he shall save it. Meaning: the individual who would—or 'should wish to'—save his life shall lose it. Exactly what is it that he wishes to save? Answer: his life, that is, himself...This man clings to that sinful life of his, holding on to it tenaciously...On the other hand, whoever loses his life 'for my sake,' he shall save it. One loses his life in the present sense by devoting oneself completely to Christ, to the service of those in need, to the gospel (Cf. Mark 8:35). Note that Christ lays claim to absolute devotion. This proves that he regards himself as Lord of all, and that the evangelist was fully aware of this! The person who offers this devotion saves his life, that is, his soul, or as we can also say, *himself*...It is only by losing oneself—looking away from self in order to serve the Master and his 'little ones' (Cf. Matt. 25:40)—that one can ever be saved...For the sinner salvation is impossible apart from obedience to this rule.[149]

Jesus never taught that one could become a Christian and

then later make a secondary 'discipleship' commitment to him, as if there were two levels of Christianity. But this is widely taught today. In fact, it is the dominant view of mainstream evangelicalism. Jesus, however, never made a distinction between being a Christian and a disciple. He used both terms interchangeably. According to Jesus, if one is not a disciple he is not a Christian. When he calls men to himself he calls them to a discipleship commitment—to take up a cross to crucify self and follow him. Scripture teaches that all who truly belong to Christ have done this: 'Now those who belong to Christ Jesus have crucified the flesh with its passions and desires' (Gal. 5:24). There are other examples in the teaching and evangelism of Jesus which highlight this truth.

Matthew 11:28-30: The Yoke

> Come to Me, all who are weary and heavy–laden, and I will give you rest. Take My yoke upon you, and learn from Me, for I am gentle and humble in heart; and you shall find rest for your souls. For My yoke is easy, and My load is light.

In Mark 8 and Luke 14 Jesus uses the image of the cross in describing discipleship. In Matthew 11, he uses the image of a yoke. The yoke was used to harness animals, to bring them into submission, so that they could be used in labor. In this passage, Jesus issues an invitation, a condition and a promise. The invitation is 'come to me,' the promise is 'rest' and the condition is 'take my yoke upon you.'

Man is restless and burdened. Why? Because he is ruled by self and not by God. What Jesus offers is his rest but it requires the fulfillment of a condition. We must bend our necks under his yoke and come into submission to his authority and teaching. We must be willing to adopt the same heart towards self that Jesus himself has. He tells us in this passage that he is meek and humble in heart. His whole life is dominated and governed by God and his will and interests. If we would come to him and find rest we must repudiate self and selfish interests and submit ourselves to Jesus as Lord—to yield to his yoke, his authority and control. James Montgomery Boice makes these observations on the meaning of Christ's yoke:

> In one of Jesus' most important sayings about discipleship...the Lord pictures discipleship as putting on a yoke. This suggests a number of things, but chiefly it suggests submission to Christ for His assigned work. It is the picture of an animal yoked to others as well as to a plow.
>
> A yoke is also the connection between submission and subjection. 'Submit' comes from the two Latin words *sub* (meaning 'under') and *mitto, mittere* (meaning 'to put' or 'place'). So submission means putting oneself under the authority of another. 'Subject' also comes from two Latin words, in this case *sub* (meaning 'under') and *iacto, iactare* (meaning 'cast' or 'throw'). It means being put under the authority of another. In other words, although the first word has an active sense (I put myself under another's authority) and the second word has a passive sense (I am placed under that authority), the idea is nevertheless essentially the same. Moreover, it is connected with 'yoke' in this way. In ancient times it was customary for a ruler, when he had conquered a new people or territory, to place a staff across two upright poles, perhaps four feet off the ground, and require the captured people to pass under it. By this act they passed under his yoke or submitted to his authority. When Jesus used this image He was saying that to follow Him was to submit to Him. It was to receive Him as Lord of one's life.[150]

John 12:24-26: The Grain of Wheat

> Truly, truly, I say to you, unless a grain of wheat falls into the earth and dies, it remains by itself alone; but if it dies it bears much fruit. He who loves his life loses it; and he who hates his life in this world shall keep it to life eternal. If anyone serves

Me, let him follow Me; and where I am, there shall My servant also be; if anyone serves Me, the Father will honor him.

Jesus gives us yet another word picture to describe his own life and attitude and that of the true Christian. He describes himself as a grain of wheat. He is using a principle drawn from the physical world to teach a spiritual truth. What is that principle? Fruitfulness and life are born out of death. It is only when the grain of wheat falls into the ground and dies that it will produce fruit. The Son of Man went to the cross to die resulting in much spiritual fruit for the kingdom of God.

Through this word picture Jesus reveals the attitude he had towards his own life. His life was not lived unto himself but for the sake of others—first and foremost, his Father.

Jesus applies this principle to all who would be his followers. I can have one of two attitudes towards my life in this world: I can love it or I can hate it. Jesus says that if I love my life I will lose it, but if I hate it I will keep it to life eternal. Again, we must understand the meaning of the word hate here. Nothing is to take priority over God and his will and kingdom in our hearts. Everything else is to be *loved less*. Our lives are not to be our highest priority. We are not here to live for ourselves but for him. If I love my life more than I love Christ and his cause I will lose it. This word *lose* is the same word Jesus uses in Mark 8 to mean perish. He is speaking about eternal death.

I must become, in a figurative sense, a grain of wheat which falls into the ground and dies. I must stop living for myself and this world and commit myself unreservedly to Christ—to love him supremely and to serve him exclusively. If I do not do this Jesus says I will perish. The apostle Paul writes of this in Romans 12:1 where he exhorts believers to continually offer themselves to God as living sacrifices: 'I urge you therefore brethren by the mercies of God to present your bodies a living and holy sacrifice, acceptable to God, which is your spiritual service of worship.' F.F. Bruce makes these comments on John 12:24:

The principle stated in verse 24 is of wide application; in particular, if it is true of Jesus, it must be true of his followers. They too must be prepared to renounce present interests for the sake of a future inheritance. This is a Johannine counterpart to the Synoptic saying about the disciple's obligation to take up his cross and follow his Master (cf. Mark 8:34-38). To love one's life here means to give it priority over the interests of God's kingdom; similarly to hate one's life is to give priority over it to the interests of God's kingdom.[151]

D.A. Carson gives these insightful observations:

But if the principle modeled by the seed—that death is the necessary condition for the generation of life—is peculiarly applicable to Jesus, in a slightly different way it is properly applied to all of Jesus' followers...The movement of thought in this passage runs from Jesus' uniquely fruitful death (the death of one seed producing many living seeds) to the mandated death of Jesus' followers as the necessary condition of their *own* life. The person who *loves his own life will lose it*: it could not be otherwise, for to love one's life is a fundamental denial of God's sovereignty, of God's rights, and a brazen elevation of self to the apogee of one's perception, and therefore an idolatrous focus on self, which is the heart of all sin. Such a person loses his life, *i.e.* causes his own perdition. By contrast, the one *who hates his life* (the love/hate contrast reflects a Semitic idiom that articulates fundamental preference, not hatred on some absolute scale...) *will keep it for eternal life* (*cf.* Mk. 8:35 par.—which also follows a passion prediction). This person denies himself, or, to use another of Jesus' metaphors, takes up his cross daily (Mk.. 8:34 par.), *i.e.* he chooses not to pander to self–interest but at the deepest level of his being declines to make himself the focus of his interest and perception, thereby *dying*.

A second contrast emerges in v. 25. The man who hates his life *in this world* will keep it *for eternal life*...These choices cannot be acts of mere self–abnegation. Self must be displaced by another; the endless, shameless focus on self must be displaced by focus on Jesus Christ, who is the supreme revelation of God.[152]

The theme of John 12 is fruit. It is one of the most important themes in all the New Testament:

- Romans 7:4 states that a believer is united to Christ for the ultimate purpose of bearing fruit unto God.
- In John 12 Jesus defines the conditions necessary for union with him in order that that fruit might be produced: a death to self and commitment to Christ to be his follower or disciple.
- John 15:8 says that we are to bear much fruit and so *prove* to be Christ's disciple. Only a disciple can bear fruit. And a true disciple is one who has met the conditions set forth by Jesus in Luke 14, Mark 8, Matthew 11 and John 12.
- Romans 6:22 states that fruit can only come from a heart and life that is wholly consecrated to God: 'But now having been freed from sin and enslaved to God, you derive your benefit (fruit), resulting in sanctification, and the outcome eternal life.'

Discipleship is the essence of true Christianity. All who would come into the kingdom of God must submit their lives to Christ as his disciple to be his follower. This is likewise seen in the commission that Christ gives his disciples in Matthew 28:19–20 :

All authority in heaven and hearth has been given to Me. Go therefore and make disciples of all nations, baptizing them in the name of the Father and the Son and the Holy Spirit, teaching them to observe all that I commanded you, And lo I am with you always even to the end of the age.

This passage is known as the Great Commission—the Savior's commission to his followers to go into all the world

and 'make disciples.' Jesus has already defined the word
disciple in Luke 14. Therefore the word will retain the same
meaning in Matthew 28. He is commissioning his followers to
carry on the same ministry that he has been engaged in—that
of bringing men and women to himself through the preaching
of the gospel. To 'make disciples' is to bring men and women
to the commitment defined by Jesus in Luke 14. It means to
make converts. We are told then to baptize *them* and teach
them. Who does the word *them* refer to? Obviously to those
who have been 'made disciples' or converts. We are to make
disciples and then baptize and teach them. An illustration of
this kind of evangelism is the rich young ruler.

The Rich Young Ruler

And as He was setting out on a journey, a man ran up to Him
and knelt before Him and began asking Him, 'Good teacher,
what shall I do to inherit eternal life?' And Jesus said to him,
'Why do you call Me good? No one is good except God
alone. You know the commandments, Do not murder, Do
not commit adultery, Do not steal, do not bear false witness,
Do not defraud, Honor your father and mother. And he said
to him, 'Teacher I have kept all these things from my youth
up.'
      And looking at him, Jesus felt a love for him, and said to
him, 'One thing you lack: go and sell all you possess and give
to the poor and you shall have treasure in heaven, and come
follow Me.' But at these words his face fell and he went away
grieved, for he was one who owned much property (Mk.
10:17–22).

This young man comes earnestly seeking the way of eternal
life. He specifically asks Jesus what he must do to be
saved. Jesus tells him that he lacks one thing. He must sell all
he possesses, give the proceeds to the poor, and follow him.
Again we are confronted with this key word—*follow*. This is
the same command Jesus gives the multitudes in Luke
14: 'Whoever does not take up his cross and *follow Me* cannot

be My disciple...No one of you can be My disciple who does not give up all his own possessions' (Lk. 14:27,33). If this young man would enter the kingdom of God and inherit eternal life he must forsake all and follow Christ. Walter Chantry makes the following comments:

> Often Christ turned crowds away by insisting that 'whosoever he be of you that forsaketh not all that he hath, he cannot be My disciple' (Lk. 14:33). He was not speaking of abundant life nor of 'victorious' giants of the faith...He demanded this turning from everything to himself as a condition of discipleship for everyone. The young ruler would turn from earthly riches to heavenly or he would cling to earthly riches and perish...The sinner must know that Jesus will not be a Savior to any man who refuses to bow to him as Lord...Christ knew nothing of the man–made twentieth–century suggestion that taking Jesus as Lord is optional. For him it was no second step which is essential for great blessings but unnecessary for entering God's kingdom. The altered message of today has deceived men and women by convincing them that Jesus will gladly be a Savior even to those who refuse to follow him as Lord. It simply is not the truth! Jesus' invitation to salvation is, 'Come, follow me'...Practical acknowledgment of Jesus' Lordship, yielding to his rule by following is the very fibre of saving faith...Believing is obeying. Without obedience, you shall not see life! Unless you bow to Christ's scepter you will not receive the benefits of Christ's sacrifice. That is just what Jesus said to the ruler.[153]

Jesus put his finger on the young man's idol and demanded that he forsake it if he would inherit eternal life. Jesus did not tell the rich young ruler simply to 'believe' in him. He commanded him to become a disciple, to follow him. This is always Jesus' message in evangelism, a call to discipleship. Thus, in Matthew 28:18–20 he is commissioning his disciples to follow his example in calling men to repentance, faith and discipleship.

Matthew 7:13-24: Beware of False Prophets

> Enter the narrow gate; for the gate is wide and the way is broad that leads to destruction and many are those who enter by it. For the gate is small, and the way is narrow that leads to life, and few are those who find it. Beware of the false prophets, who come to you in sheep's clothing, but inwardly are ravenous wolves (Mt. 7:13–15).

Christ warns that the gate is strait and the way is narrow that leads to life. It is narrow because Christ is the only way and because the conditions required for those who would enter are difficult. We do well to heed Jesus' words of warning in Matthew 7: 'Beware of the false prophets, who come to you in sheep's clothing, but inwardly are ravenous wolves' (Mt. 7:15). False prophets proclaim a false message resulting in false assurance. They dilute the demands of the gospel by making the gate wide and the way broad. Such teachers and preachers may *acknowledge* Christ as Lord, by affirming his deity, but deny that a commitment *to* him as Lord is necessary for salvation. But acknowledging the title or position of Jesus theologically and *submitting to* him *as* Lord are very different. Jesus tells us that those who profess his deity without a corresponding submission of life will not enter heaven. Only those who do the will of God will enter heaven:

> Not everyone who says to Me, 'Lord, Lord,' will enter the kingdom of heaven; but he who does the will of My Father who is in heaven. Many will say to Me on that day, 'Lord, Lord, did we not prophecy in your name, and in Your name cast out demons, and in Your name perform many miracles?' And I will declare to them, 'I never knew you; depart from Me, you who practice lawlessness.'

The people Jesus mentions are sincere and orthodox in their view of Christ but they are lost. Jesus says the reason is that they practice lawlessness. 1 John 3:4 says, 'Sin is lawlessness.'

Lawlessness is a heart of rebellion against God. A heart of self–will and self–rule. These people profess Christ as Lord but they do not submit to him *as* Lord to do his will. In preaching the gospel we must call men to Christ, but in doing so, we must impress upon them what that will mean. If we minimize Christ's demands for repentance and faith we will in effect be wolves in sheep's clothing—false prophets declaring to men a wide gate and a broad way of salvation. Martyn Lloyd–Jones gives this warning about the false prophets of Matthew 7:

> We are told at the very outset of this way of life, before we start on it that if we would walk along it there are certain things which must be left outside, behind us. There is no room for them because we have to start by passing through a strait and narrow gate...The first thing we leave behind us is what is called worldliness. We leave behind the crowd and the way of the world...Our Lord is warning us against the danger of an easy salvation, against the tendency to say—Just come to Christ as you are and all is going to be well. No, the gospel tells us at the outset that it is going to be difficult. It means a radical break with the world...Yes, but still narrower and still straiter, if we really want to come into this way of life, we have to leave our 'self' outside. And it is there of course that we come to the greatest stumbling–block of all. It is one thing to leave the world, and the way of the world, but the most important thing in a sense is to leave our self outside. Have no illusion about this...for he who would enter by this gate must say goodbye to self. It is a life of self-abasement, self humiliation. 'If any man will come after Me'—what happens? Let him deny himself (the first thing always), and take up his cross and follow Me. But self denial, denial of self, does not mean refraining from various pleasures and things that we may like. It means to deny our very right to ourself. We leave our self outside and go through the gate saying, 'Yet not I but Christ liveth in Me.'
> In the same way it (the false prophet's teaching) does not

emphasize repentance in any real sense. It has a very wide gate leading to salvation and a very broad way leading to heaven. You need not feel much of your own sinfulness; you need not be aware of the blackness of your own heart. You just decide for Christ and rush in with the crowd and your name is put down and is one of the large number of decisions reported by the press.

Repentance means that you realize that you are a guilty vile sinner in the presence of God; that you deserve the wrath and punishment of God, that you are hell–bound. It means that you begin to realize that this thing called sin is in you; that you long to get rid of it, and that you turn your back on it in every shape and form. You renounce the world whatever the cost, the world in its mind and outlook as well as its practice, and you deny yourself, and take up the cross and go after Christ. Your nearest and dearest and the whole world may call you a fool, or say you have religious mania. You may have to suffer financially, but it makes no difference. That is repentance. The false prophet does not put it like that. He heals 'the hurt of the daughter of My people slightly,' simply saying that it is all right and that you have but to come to Christ, 'follow Christ,' or 'become a Christian.'[154]

Jesus' Definition of the Word Disciple

The yoke, the cross, the grain of wheat, a follower, a servant— these are all terms used by Jesus to describe his radical teaching on what it means to truly know him. But much of his teaching today is misinterpreted, misunderstood or misapplied. Many evangelical teachers today view discipleship strictly as the process of sanctification or a second, deeper commitment, not as that which pertains to entering the kingdom of God.

The Greek word for disciple is *mathetes,* which means a learner. However, Jesus broadens the term beyond its basic Greek meaning. We must define the word by his teaching. Disciples in the day of Jesus committed themselves to a teacher to learn his philosophy. But Jesus is not calling men to a philosophy but to himself in an exclusive love relationship. A disciple of Jesus will be a learner, but his disciple will be much more. He will be a *follower*, one who has denied self, taken up a cross and forsaken all to live for Christ and his kingdom. According to Jesus, only a disciple is a true Christian. The teaching of Jesus must be our defining standard.

The Demands of Discipleship and the Gospel

The call of Jesus is a call to repentance and conversion. As was pointed out at the beginning of our study, we were created by God to fulfil a specific purpose. All things have been created 'by Him and *for* Him' (Col. 1:16). He, himself, is to be the supreme purpose for our existence and the object of our love (Ex. 20:2–3; Mt. 22:37). Man was created to live under God's authority, to love him supremely, and to live in obedience to his will. Our fundamental problem, however, is that we do not live this way. We have rebelled against our Creator and do not live to fulfil his will but our own. The bible calls this sin. In the chapter on sin we noted that the first and foremost issue in defining sin is not with particular acts of behavior but the disposition of the heart in relation to the person of God himself. Therefore, since repentance means turning from sin, the first issue to deal with in turning will relate to our heart relationship with the person of God and then specific issues of sinful behavior.

In the passages we have looked at, Jesus is defining and applying the truth of repentance. He explains what it means in practical terms. The specific issues mentioned in Luke 14— other relationships, one's own life, possessions—are potential idols which can displace God from his rightful place of preeminence in the heart. They must be torn down and cast away. Jonathan Edwards underscores this when he says: 'One great thing he (Jesus) aimed at in redemption, was to deliver them from their idols, and bring them to God.'[155] Therefore, any man who comes to Christ must forsake all (Lk. 14:33), submit his life to him as Lord and First Love and follow him. This is the nature of repentance. It underlines again that salvation means more than deliverance from the guilt and condemnation of sin. It is restoration to a *relationship* with God so that we may fulfil the purpose for which we were created: to love, worship, serve, obey and glorify him. J.I. Packer makes this point about Christ's call to repentance:

> Repentance is more than just sorrow for the past; repentance is a change of mind and heart, a new life of denying self and serving the Savior as King in self's place...More than once Christ deliberately called attention to the radical break with the past that *repentance* involves. Luke 9:23,24—'If any man will come after Me, let him deny himself and take up his cross and follow Me, whosoever will lose his life for My sake the same (but only he) will save it.' Luke 14:26,33—'If any man come to Me and hate not his father and mother and wife and children and brethren and sisters yea and his own life also (i.e., put them all decisively second in his esteem) he cannot be my disciple...whosoever he be of you that forsaketh not all that he hath, he cannot be My disciple.' The *repentance* that Christ requires of His people consists in a settled refusal to set any limit to the claims which He may make on their lives.[156]

The New Testament call of Christ to discipleship is in principle the same call God gave during the Old Testament days of Ezekiel. It is a call to repentance and conversion—a turning from and forsaking of idolatry and sin:

> Then some of the elders of Israel came to me and sat down before me. And the word of the Lord came to me saying, 'Son of man, these men have set up their idols in their hearts, and have put right before their faces the stumbling block of their iniquity. Should I be consulted by them at all? Therefore speak to them and tell them, Thus says the Lord God, Any

man of the house of Israel who sets up his idols in his heart, puts right before his face the stumbling block of his iniquity, and then comes to the prophet, I the Lord will be brought to give him an answer in the matter in view of the multitude of his idols, in order to lay hold of the hearts of the house of Israel who are estranged from Me through all their idols.

Therefore say to the house of Israel, Thus says the Lord God, Repent and turn away from your idols, and turn your faces away from all your abominations.'

Therefore I will judge you, O house of Israel, each according to his conduct declares the Lord God. Repent and turn away from all your transgressions, so that iniquity may not become a stumbling block to you. Cast away from you all your transgressions which you have committed, and make yourselves a new heart and a new spirit! For why will you die, O house of Israel? For I have no pleasure in the death of anyone who dies, declares the Lord God. Therefore, repent and live (Ez. 14:1–6, 18:30–32).

If a man does not become a disciple as defined by Jesus he will perish because he has never truly repented. Acts 11:26 tells us that 'the disciples were called Christians first in Antioch.' Before the term Christian was coined they were called disciples. James Montgomery Boice offers this warning concerning the salvation teachings of Jesus:

There is a fatal defect in the life of Christ's church in the twentieth century: a lack of true discipleship. Discipleship means forsaking everything to follow Christ. But for many of today's supposed Christians—perhaps the majority—it is the case that while there is much talk about Christ and even much furious activity, there is actually very little following of Christ Himself. And that means in some circles there is very little genuine Christianity. Many who fervently call Him 'Lord, Lord' are not Christians (Matthew 7:21)...There are several reasons that the situation I have described is common in today's church. The first is a defective theology that has crept over us like a deadening fog. This theology separates faith from discipleship and grace from obedience. It teaches that Jesus can be received as one's Savior without being received as one's Lord...Discipleship in not a supposed second step in Christianity, as if one first became a believer in Jesus and then, if he chooses, a disciple. From the beginning, discipleship is involved in what it means to be a Christian....Is 'faith' minus commitment a true biblical faith?...If faith without works is dead—how much truer is it that faith without commitment is dead...True faith involves these elements: knowledge...heart response...and commitment, without which 'faith' is no different from the assent of the demons who 'believe...and shudder' (James 2:19). [157]

A.W. Tozer makes these comments:

The sinner is actually a rebel against properly constituted authority. That is what makes sin—sin. We are rebels. We are sons of disobedience. Sin is the breaking of the law and we are in rebellion and we are fugitives *from* the just laws of God while we are sinners. The root of sin is rebellion against law, rebellion against God. Does not the sinner say, I belong to myself. I owe allegiance to no one unless I choose to give it. That is the essence of sin. Thus in repentance, we reverse that relationship and we fully submit to the Word of God and the will of God as obedient children. We have no basis to believe that we can come casually and sprightly to the Lord Jesus and say, I have come for some help, Lord Jesus. I understand that you are the Savior so I am going to believe and be saved and then I am going to turn away and think about the other matters of lordship and allegiance and obedience at some other time in the future.

I warn you, you will not get help from Him in that way for the Lord will not save those whom He cannot command. He will not divide His offices. You cannot believe on a half Christ. We take Him for what He is, the anointed Savior and Lord who is King of Kings and Lord of Lords.[158]

The Bible unequivocally teaches that surrender to the Lordship of Christ is a necessary condition for salvation. This is seen not only in the teaching of Jesus but is also stated or implied in the following verses:

> For to this end Christ died and lived *again*, that He might be Lord both of the dead and of the living (Romans 14:9).
>
> And He died for all, that they who live should no longer live for themselves, but for Him who died and rose again on their behalf (2 Cor. 5:15).
>
> But now having been freed from sin and enslaved to God, you derive your benefit, resulting in sanctification, and the outcome, eternal life (Rom. 6:22).
>
> That if you confess with your mouth Jesus *as* Lord, and believe in your heart that God raised Him from the dead, you shall be saved (Rom. 10:9).
>
> For they themselves report about us what kind of a reception we had with you, and how you turned to God from idols to serve a living and true God (1 Thes. 1:9).

The salvation teachings of Jesus encompass the great themes of divine sovereignty, union with himself, justification, sanctification, regeneration, adoption, repentance, faith and conversion. The gospel of the Reformation is the gospel of Jesus, of Paul and scripture.

~ 12 ~

The Gospel and Evangelicalism

I solemnly charge you in the presence of God and of Christ Jesus, who is to judge the living and the dead, and by His appearing and His kingdom: preach the word; be ready in season and out of season; reprove, rebuke, exhort, with great patience and instruction...Be sober in all things, endure hardship, do the work of an evangelist, fulfill your ministry (2 Timothy 4:1-2, 6)

Having examined the gospel of the scriptures, the teaching of Jesus, and the position of the Reformers and Reformed theologians on the application and appropriation of salvation some serious concerns must be raised about the gospel which is being presented by some evangelicals in our day.

We will look at three doctrinal positions held within evangelical circles. The difference between them is not over justification, but with the nature of salvation and saving faith. All agree that justification is by faith alone in Christ alone. All are orthodox in their definition of justification—the sufficiency of the atonement of Christ and imputed righteousness. How then do they differ? The divergence of opinion has been brought into focus by the current lordship salvation debate.

We will call those in the first camp 'pro–lordship'. They hold to the inseparability of justification and sanctification in the salvation experience, teaching that sanctification is the inevitable result of union with Christ and the evidence of saving faith. They teach that saving faith involves not only trust in Christ as Savior but also repentance and commitment to Christ as Lord.

The salvation doctrine of the second camp is characterized by the teaching called 'easy–believism.' These teachers define saving faith as trust in Christ as Savior only. They strongly deny the necessity for repentance and submission to Christ as Lord for salvation. They teach that sanctification, while desirable, is not absolutely necessary in the overall experience of salvation. They define salvation as justification and imputed righteousness alone.

The third position is the one I want to focus our attention on in the rest of this chapter. Many who call themselves Reformed hold this position, one which I feel is both subtle in its error and dangerous. Those who are in this third camp agree in a broad sense with *most* of Reformation theology. The danger is not in what is agreed upon but in what is denied. These teachers rightly condemn the antinomian emphasis of 'easy–believism' and are emphatic in their insistence that saving faith will result in a life characterized by sanctification. So far so good. But their definition of saving faith is incomplete. They do not teach repentance as an essential corrollary to saving faith but rather as a *fruit* of faith and justification. Therefore to call of men to Christ is to call them to faith alone and not to repentance and faith. So when an individual is 'saved,' it is through a faith they have defined as knowledge (an intellectual understanding of the facts related to the work of Christ), assent (intellectually concluding that the facts are true) and trust in the person and work of Christ (coming to the settled conviction that these facts are true for me personally). But this faith is void of any call to repentance and submission to Christ as Lord. It is not that they deny the necessity for repentance but they insist it occurs only *after* one has believed. Many Reformed people hold to the same weak view of faith as those in the camp of 'easy–believism'. Its focus is exclusively upon the work of Christ in atonement and on imputed righteousness. Men in both camps are silent on many of the important teachings of Jesus regarding the nature of salvation. The issues of discipleship and lordship are not viewed as teachings which have direct bearing on what it means to come into a relationship with Christ and thereby to enter the kingdom of God. Saving faith is defined as trusting Christ as Savior only. Lordship, then, is relegated to the *process* of sanctification. In this sense there is an affirmation of lordship but not in the initial exercise of faith.

Let's be clear, saving faith *does* involve knowledge of, assent to the facts of the gospel and trust in Christ, but this is not all that is involved in the biblical teaching on faith. Faith defined as trust in Christ as Savior only, is *not* biblical saving faith. It is insufficient. It omits an equally important element in faith, namely, commitment—as Jesus defines it in his discipleship teachings in Luke 14 and Mark 8. James Montgomery Boice points this out:

> Is 'faith' minus commitment a true biblical faith?...If faith without works is dead—how much truer is it that faith without commitment is dead...True faith involves these elements: knowledge...heart response...and commitment, without which 'faith' is no different from the assent of the demons who 'believe...and shudder' (James 2:19).[159]

J.I. Packer says:

> That man should not separate what God has joined is a truth about more than marriage. God has joined the three offices of prophet (teacher), priest, and king in the mediatorial role of Jesus Christ, and directs us in the Bible to relate positively to them all. God has joined faith and repentance as the two facets of response to the Savior and made it clear that turning to Christ means turning from sin and letting ungodliness go. Biblical teaching on faith joins credence, commitment, and communion; it exhibits Christian believing as not only knowing facts about Christ, but also coming to him in personal trust to worship, love and serve him...'Lordship

salvation' is a name for the view that upholds these unities...It is no more, just as it is no less, than the mainstream Protestant consensus on the nature of justifying faith...Simple assent to the gospel, divorced from a transforming commitment to the living Christ, is by biblical standards less than faith, and less than saving, and to elicit only assent of this kind would be to secure only false conversions.[160]

As noted earlier, we need to distinguish between discipleship as a commitment and discipleship as a process. It is both. It is precisely the same distinction, which we examined, that John Murray makes regarding definitive and progressive sanctification. When Jesus calls men he calls them first ·to a *commitment* of discipleship. That commitment results in union with him and will *then* produce a life of growth in discipleship or sanctification. But unless the initial commitment is made there will be no union with Christ, no new life, the Holy Spirit will not indwell the heart and the individual will not be converted and therefore there will be no sanctification. While those in the third camp reject the teaching that one can have saving faith without the works of sanctification, they object strenuously to the fact that a lordship/discipleship *commitment* is an integral part of such faith. But to teach that commitment to Christ as Lord occurs only after one has been brought into a saving relationship with him is to distort the meaning of saving faith. Commitment to Christ as Lord is an integral part of repentance and cannot be separated from the initial act of saving faith. Repentance is not the fruit of a relationship with God but a condition for entering the relationship. It is a repentant–faith that saves and unites us to Christ and produces sanctification. Justification *is* by faith alone, but we must accurately define that faith. The Westminster Confession states that an essential part of the exercise of saving faith is the receiving of Christ as Sanctification: 'The principal acts of saving faith are accepting, receiving, and resting upon Christ alone for justification, sanctification and eternal life, by virtue of the covenant of grace.'[161] And John Owen points out that the works of sanctification are rooted in a life that is submitted to Christ: 'All obedience unto Christ proceeds from an express subjection of our souls and consciences unto Him.'[162] Since receiving Christ as sanctification is an essential element of saving faith and sanctification must begin with submission to Christ, then submission to Christ as Lord is an essential aspect of saving faith.

The definition of faith as trust in Christ as Savior only focuses exclusively on justification. This is shortsighted. It fails to emphasize the biblical view of salvation as deliverance from sin. Salvation is applied to men's hearts as they receive Christ and are united to him through repentance and faith. As we have seen, this is the consistent emphasis of Reformed teaching. John Murray confirms this:

> The interdependence of faith and repentance can be readily seen when we remember that faith is faith in Christ for salvation from sin. But if faith is directed to salvation from sin, there must be hatred of sin and the desire to be saved from it. Such hatred of sin involves repentance which essentially consists in turning from sin unto God.[163]

The teaching of faith alone was emphasized by the Reformers to counteract the Roman Catholic emphasis on the necessity for the sacraments and good works to attain justification. But to define the Reformation teaching of faith alone as trust in Christ without repentance and commitment to him is a distortion of both the Reformation teaching and the gospel message. Faith alone means faith without the merit of works, not repentance. The Bible always presents repentance as a corollary to faith in receiving Christ for salvation.

Dead Faith or Living Faith

According to scripture, living faith produces fruit or works while dead faith does not. James speaks of dead faith which he calls non–saving because it does not result in sanctification (Js. 2:14–21). What then, is the difference between faith that produces works and faith that does not?

Paul gives us the answer in Romans 6 where he says that it is impossible for one who is truly justified to continue living in sin. Why? The issue is union with Christ. The life united to Christ possesses a certain kind of heart and produces a certain kind of behavior. This is a truth we touched on in our discussion of sanctification and is explained in Romans 6:22: 'But now having been freed from sin and enslaved to God, you derive your benefit (fruit), resulting in sanctification, and the outcome eternal life.' Paul teaches that the person who bears fruit in sanctification has been freed from sin as a ruling power and has become *enslaved* to God. He has been brought into subjection to God. That word enslaved, as previously pointed out, is the Greek word *doulos.* It speaks of the relationship of a servant to a Lord or Master. When an individual is united to Christ through repentance and faith he becomes a slave to God through Christ. Therefore, the essential difference between saving and non–saving faith is not only trust in Christ as Savior but surrender and commitment to Christ as Lord.

Christ has accomplished a complete and finished work, but in order for that salvation to be applied to the individual life, Christ himself must be appropriated. Saving faith defined as trust in Christ without repentance and commitment is incomplete, insufficient. Such faith will *not* produce a life of sanctification and good works because the individual will not be in union with Christ—the heart is left in rebellion against God. The mind may embrace the facts concerning Christ, but the life has not truly embraced the person of Christ. These Reformed teachers who promote an 'easy–believism' definition of faith are committed to the Reformation principle of scripture alone (*sola scriptura*). Yet, by misinterpreting the fundamental teachings of Christ, they unwittingly promote an antinomian message even while affirming the truth of sanctification (as a process). By appealing to men to trust in Jesus as Savior only without repenting, the message offered assures them of eternal salvation from hell but not sin. If a man does not yield to Christ as Lord he is in rebellion against him and stands opposed to him as Lord. The words of Thomas Watson bear repeating: 'Knowledge without repentance will be but a torch to light men to hell.'[164]

Many today have departed from the biblical gospel. While Roman Catholicism has distorted the meaning of justification, much of evangelicalism has distorted the meaning of saving faith. We do well to heed Dabney's warning:

> The selfishness and guilty conscience of man prompt him powerfully to look to the Saviour exclusively as a remedy for guilt, even when awakened by the Spirit. The first and most urgent want of the soul, convicted of its guilt and danger, is impunity. Hence, the undue prevalence, even in preaching, of that view of Christ which holds Him up as expiation only. We have seen...what I regard as the dangerous statement, that the true believer, in embracing Christ, first receives Him only in His priestly office! The faith which does no more than this, is but partial, and can bear but spurious fruits. Is not this the explanation of much of that defective and spurious religion with which the Church is cursed? The man who is savingly wrought upon by the Holy Ghost, is made to feel that his bondage under corruption is an evil as inexorable and dreadful as the penal curse of the law. He needs and desires Christ in His prophetic and kingly offices, as much as in His priestly. His faith 'receives Him as He is offered in the gospel;' that is, as a 'Saviour of His people from their sins.'[165]

Assurance

So what about assurance? Is there any? Romans 8:1 assures us that for all that are 'in Christ Jesus' there is no condemnation. All who have savingly believed in Christ have the gift of eternal life (Jn. 3:16) and can *know* they have it (1 Jn. 5:12–13). But scripture also warns those who have professed faith in Christ against a 'dead faith' that is no more than words. It is not those who *profess* Christ but those who *possess* him who can know they have the gift of eternal life: 'He who *has* the Son has life; he who does not have the Son of God does not have the life' (1 Jn. 5:12; Jn. 1:12). Without practical holiness, no man will see the Lord (Heb. 12:15). Peter, Paul, James, John and Jesus all warned against a false or spurious faith (2 Pet. 1:10; 2 Cor. 13:5; Js. 2:14–26; 1 Jn. 2:3–4; Jn. 8:30–34) and the repeated admonition of scripture is for self examination— to make our calling and election sure: 'Test yourselves to see if you are in the faith; examine yourselves! Or do you not recognize this about yourselves, that Jesus Christ is in you— unless you fail the test?' (2 Cor. 13:5).

Assurance in scripture is given to that one who has truly received Christ, evidenced by the manifestation of his character in that life. The example of the Pharisees should sober us. It is possible to have orthodoxy of doctrine, outward religious conformity and be lost.

It is not the place of a preacher or teacher to give assurance of salvation to anyone. That is the right and ministry of the Holy Spirit. We may assure an individual that if he comes to Christ in repentance and faith he will be received: 'All that the Father gives Me shall come to Me, and the one who comes to Me I will certainly not cast out' (Jn. 6:37). This is Christ's own promise. But it is fulfilled only to those who come on his terms.

We have a tremendous responsibility to warn men of spurious or dead faith and to lift up the biblical standard of salvation. This is the purpose of the book of 1 John. John tells his readers that a profession of faith in Christ is meaningless without a corresponding holiness of life. Those who know Christ *will* keep his commandments (1 Jn. 2:3–4). John tells his readers how to test themselves to see if they really know God, are 'in Christ' and therefore abide in him: Do you walk as Jesus walked (1 Jn. 2:5-6)?

We have every right biblically to tell men that if they are not holy, if they are not being conformed to Jesus in character, but are characterized instead by habitual sin, then they have never been justified. If there is no holiness, there is no *saving* faith. This is especially true in our day of easy–believism. James Montgomery Boice has voiced a concern that multitudes of professing Christians may actually be deluded by a false faith. He pleads for self–examination:

> It is not only a false theology that has encouraged this fatal lack of discipleship. The error is also due to the absence of what the older devotional writers called a 'self–examined life.' Most Westerners live in a tragically mindless environment. Life is too fast, and our contact with other persons too impersonal for any real thought or reflection. Even in the church we are far more often encouraged to join this committee, back this project, or serve on this board than we are counseled to examine our relationship to God and His Son Jesus Christ. So long as we are performing for the church, few question whether our profession is genuine or spurious. *But sermons should suggest that members of a church may not actually be saved, although they are members.* Teachers should stress that a personal, self-denying, costly, and persistent following of Christ is necessary if a person is to be acknowledged by Jesus in the last day...In the absence of this teaching millions drift on, assuming that because they have made a verbal acknowledgment of Christ ten, twenty, or even thirty years ago and have done nothing terribly bad since, they are Christians, when actually they may be far from Christ, devoid of grace, and in danger of perishing forever (emphasis mine).[166]

Dr. Boice suggests that preachers preach with the objective of bringing men to self–examination, to question the genuineness of their profession. This is what Paul exhorted the Corinthians to do: 'Test yourselves to see if you are in the faith; examine yourselves! Or do you not recognize this about yourselves, that Jesus Christ is in you—unless indeed you fail the test' (2 Cor. 13:5)? The seriousness of Jesus' teaching on

discipleship in contrast to the current message of easy–
believism makes the call to self–examination all the more
urgent and necessary. Better occasional self doubt than
eternal deception. We must be faithful to present a true and
complete gospel, to assure men that God will receive them if
they come—*on his terms*. The Reformers did not shrink from
challenging men to examine their lives—to make their calling
and election sure. Note this exhortation from Thomas
Cranmer:

> All Holy Scripture agreeably beareth witness that a true lively
> faith in Christ doth bring forth good works; and therefore
> every man must examine himself diligently, to know whether
> he have the same true lively faith in his heart unfeignedly or
> not; which he shall know by the fruits thereof...A man may
> soon deceive himself, and think in his own phantasy that he by
> faith knoweth God, loveth him, feareth him, and belongeth to
> him, when in very deed he doeth nothing less...Some
> peradventure phantasy in themselves that they belong to
> God, although they live in sin; and so they come to the church,
> and shew themselves as God's dear children. But St. John
> saith plainly: 'If we say that we have any company with God,
> and walk in darkness, we do lie.'...Deceive not yourselves,
> therefore, thinking that you have faith in God, or that you
> love God, or do trust in him, or do fear him, when you live in
> sin; for then your ungodly and sinful life declareth the
> contrary, whatsoever you say or think. It pertaineth to a
> Christian man to have this true Christian faith, and to try
> himself whether he hath it or no, and to know what belongeth
> to it, and how it doth work in him...Let us therefore, good
> Christian people, try and examine our faith, what it is: let us
> not flatter ourselves, but look upon our works, and so judge
> of our faith, what it is. Christ himself speaketh of this matter,
> and saith: 'The tree is known by the fruit.'[167]

~ Conclusion ~

Even though we, or an angel from heaven, should preach to you a gospel contrary to that which we have preached to you, let him be accursed. As we have said before, so I say again now, if any man is preaching to you a gospel contrary to that which you received, let him be accursed (Galatians 1:8–9)

The Church must be bound to none other authority than unto the voice of the gospel and unto the ministry thereof (John Hooper, English Reformer).[168]

If we would be true to the Lord and to the Reformation heritage we embrace, we must take a strong stand against any ecumenical movement that is willing to compromise the biblical gospel for unity with Roman Catholicism. Rome claims that the *sola fide* teaching of the Reformation rejected all works of holiness and the need for moral transformation, and that its concept of forensic justification was a legal fiction which was anithetical to scripture. These accusations are false. While it is true that the Reformers emphasized *sola fide* in their teaching on salvation it is also clear from their writings that in doing so, they did not exclude the necessity for regeneration, sanctification, adoption, repentance, and conversion. The Reformers did not reject the proper place of works in the *overall* scheme of salvation. They simply declared that justification was not based on the *merit* of sacraments or human works but exclusively on a relationship with Christ. Given the historical context in which the Reformers lived and taught and the errors of Rome with which they had to contend, it was necessary to focus on the biblical truth of justification. But as we have stated repeatedly, justification is just one aspect of the overall message of salvation proclaimed by them. Their teaching is an affirmation of and is in conformity with the teaching of scripture on salvation.

It is also important that we stand against the corruption of the Reformation gospel by the antinomian element within evangelicalism which corrupts the biblical meaning of saving faith by denying the necessity for commitment to Christ as Lord for salvation. This directly contradicts the teaching of Christ and scripture. As evangelicals, it is possible to rightly hold orthodox views on justification (in opposition to legalism), only to fall into the heresy of antinomianism. We can espouse scripturally accurate teachings on justification and be guilty of distorting the biblical teaching on saving faith. In so doing, while we claim the theological heritage of the Reformation, in practice we may embrace teachings which deny it.

We must maintain the distinction between justification and sanctification. Justification is based upon an imputed righteousness which completely delivers from the guilt and condemnation of sin. It is the only basis for our salvation. At the same time we must emphasize the necessity for repentance and submission to Christ as Lord in the application of that salvation. What profit is there if we rightly interpret the meaning of justification and pervert the meaning of saving faith?

We must preach the *whole* counsel of God. Without a gospel call that includes repentance from sin and Christ's call to discipleship, we will be guilty of proclaiming a false or incomplete gospel. The Christ who saves and justifies cannot be appropriated apart from a faith that commits to him.

The Church and our culture are in great need of revival. If we long to see it happen we must stand against the legalism of Rome and the easy–believism of much of evangelicalism and return to the proclamation of the biblical and Reformation gospel. The Reformers *preached* the gospel. They were bold and uncompromising and witnessed the power of God in great revival. Wherever the true gospel is preached and given its place of primacy and priority, wonderful transformations occur in the lives of individuals. We need a new Reformation today—a return to the biblical gospel message and a commitment to its proclamation in the power of the Holy Spirit. Paul's words are as true today as when he first penned them:

The **Gospel** *is the* **power** *of God* **for salvation** *for everyone who believes*

ENDNOTES

[1]B.B. Warfield, *Faith & Life* (Edinburgh: Banner, 1974), pp. 174-176.

[2]D. Martyn Lloyd-Jones, *Romans: The New Man, Exposition of Chapter 6* (Grand Rapids: Zondervan, 1972), p. 218.

[3]A.A. Hodge, *Evangelical Theology* (Edinburgh: Banner, 1976), p. 274.

[4]John Murray, *Collected Writings of John Murray* (Edinburgh: Banner, 1977), pp. 219-220.

[5]John Murray, *Collected Writings of John Murray* (Edinburgh: Banner, 1977), Volume 2, p. 78.

[6]J.I. Packer, *God's Words* (Downers Grove: Inter Varsity), pp. 72-74.

[7]J.C. Ryle, *Holiness* (Cambridge: Clarke). p. 1.

[8]Jonathan Edwards, *The Works of Jonathan Edwards* (Edinburgh: Banner, 1974), Volume 2, *Men Naturally Are God's Enemies*, Sect. III, pp. 132-133.

[9]John Blanchard, *Whatever Happened to Hell?* (Evangelical Press: Durham, 1993), pp. 41-42.

[10]John Calvin, *Institutes of the Christian Religion.* Found in *The Library of Christian Classics* (Westminster: Philadelphia), Volume XIX, Book III.XXV.12, pp. 1007-8.

[11]John Calvin, *Institutes of the Christian Religion.* Found in *The Library of Christian Classics* (Philadelphia: Westminster, 1960), Volume XIX, Book III, Ch. XI.1, p. 725.

[12]John Calvin, *Institutes of the Christian Religion.* Found in *The Library of Christian Classics* (Philadelphia: Westminster, 1960), Volume XIX, Book III, Ch. XIV.5, p. 793.

[13]John Calvin, *Institutes of the Christian Religion.* Found in *The Library of Christian Classics* (Philadelphia: Westminster, 1960), Volume XIX, Book III, Ch. XI.10, pp. 736-737.

[14]Heinrich Bullinger, *Of the Holy Catholic Church.* Cited by *The Library of Christian Classics* (Philadelphia: Westminster, 1953), Volume XXIV, p. 305.

[15]Martin Luther, *The Freedom of a Christian.* Found in *Martin Luther's Basic Theological Writings*, Timothy Lull, Ed., (Minneapolis: Fortress, 1989), p. 603.

[16]John Owen, *The Works of John Owen* (Edinburgh: Banner, 1965), Volume 3, p. 516.

[17]Louis Berkhof, *Systematic Theology* (Grand Rapids: Eerdmans, 1939), p. 450.

[18]R.L. Dabney, *Lectures In Systematic Theology* (Grand Rapids: Zondervan, 1980), Lecture LI, pp. 612-613.

[19]Leon Morris, *The Apostolic Preaching of the Cross* (Grand Rapids: Eerdmans, 1972), p. 233.

[20]Huldrych Zwingli, *Commentary On True and False Religion* (Durham: Labyrinth, 1981), pp. 141–142.

[21]James Buchanan, *The Doctrine of Justification* (Edinburgh: Banner, 1961), pp. 305–306).

[22]James Buchanan, *The Doctrine of Justification* (Edinburgh: Banner, 1961), p. 319.

[23]Leon Morris, *The Apostolic Preaching of the Cross* (Grand Rapids: Eerdmans, 1955), pp. 225-226, 234-235, 249.

[24]John Murray, *Collected Writings of John Murray* (Edinburgh: Banner, 1977), Volume II, pp. 206–208.

[25]Don Kistler, Ed., *Justification By Faith Alone* (Morgan: Soli Deo Gloria, 1995), pp. 85–86.

[26]*What Still Divides Us?* A Protestant & Roman Catholic Debate, Tape #WSD-05, Roman Catholic Critique of Sola Fide, Christians United For Reformation, Anaheim, CA.

[27]John Calvin, *Institutes of the Christian Religion.* Found in *The Library of Christian Classics* (Philadelphia: Westminster, 1960), Volume XIX, Book III, Chapter XI.2–3, pp. 726–728.

[28]Martin Luther, *Epistle Sermon, Twenty–fourth Sunday After Trinity* (Lenker Edition, Vol. IX, #43–45. Found in *A Compend of Luther's Theology,* Hugh Kerr, Ed., (Philadelphia: Westminster, 1966), pp. 52–53.

[29]Thomas Cranmer, *An Homily of the Salvation of Mankind by Only Christ Our Saviour from Sin and Death Everlasting.* Found in *The Library of Christian Classics* (Philadelphia: Westminster, 1966), Volume XXVI, pp. 262, 264.

[30]Colin Brown, Ed., *Dictionary of New Testament Theology* (Grand Rapids: Zondervan, 1978), Volume III, p. 1182.

[31]Philip Melanchthon, *Love and Hope.* Found in *The Library of Christian Classics* (Philadelphia: Westminster, 1969), Volume XIX, p. 112.

[32]Thomas Cranmer, *A Short Declaration of the True, Lively and Christian Faith.* Found in *The Library of Christian Classics* (Philadelphia:

Westminster, 1966), Volume XXVI, pp. 272–273.

[33]Ludwig Ott, *Fundamentals of Catholic Dogma* (Rockford: Tan, 1974), pp. 264–265.

[34]John Murray, *Collected Writings of John Murray* (Edinburgh: Banner, 1977), Volume 2, pp. 221–222.

[35]Martin Luther, *Two Kinds of Righteousness*. Taken from *Martin Luther's Basic Theological Writings* (Minneapolis: Fortress, 1989), pp. 156–158.

[36]John Hooper, *A Declaration of Christe and His Offyce*. Found in *The Library of Christian Classics* (Philadelphia: Westminster, 1966), Volume XXVI, p. 206.

[37]*The Westminster Confession of Faith*, Chapter XII. Cited in A.A. Hodge, *The Confession of Faith* (Edinburgh: Banner, 1958), p. 191.

[38]Ludwig Ott, *Fundamentals of Catholic Dogma* (Rockford: Tan, 1974), pp. 185, 190.

[39]John Hardon, *The Question and Answer Catholic Catechism* (Garden City: Image, 1981), Questions # 401, 402, 461, 462, 1119.

[40]*The Canons and Decrees of the Council of Trent*. Found in Philip Schaff, *The Creeds of Christendom* (Grand Rapids: Baker, 1919), Canon IV, p. 119.

[41]*The Canons and Decrees of the Council of Trent*. Found in Philip Schaff, *The Creeds of Christendom* (Grand Rapids: Baker, 1910), Decree on Justification, Chapter XIV. Canon XXIX.

[42]John Hardon, *The Question and Answer Catholic Catechism* (Garden City: Image, 1981), Question #1320.

[43]*The Canons and Decrees of the Council of Trent*. Found in Philip Schaff, *The Creeds of Christendom* (Grand Rapids: Baker, 1910), Doctrine on the Sacrifice of the Mass, Chp. II, p. 180, Canon III.

[44]John Hardon, *The Question and Answer Catholic Catechism* (Garden City: Image, 1981), Questions #1265, 1269, 1277.

[45]John Knox, *A Vindication of the Doctrine That the Mass Is Idolatry*. Found in *The Works of John Owen* (Edinburgh: James Thin, 1895), Volume III, p. 56. *Language revised by William Webster*.

[46]Nicholas Ridley, *Examinations of the Eucharist*. Found in *The Library of Christian Classics* (Philadelphia: Westminster, 1966), Volume XXVI, pp. 314–315.

[47]William Marshner, *Justification by Faith*. Taken from *Reasons for Hope: Catholic Apologetics* (Front Royal: Christendom College, 1978), pp. 232–233.

[48]*The Canons and Decrees of the Council of Trent*. Found in Philip Schaff, *The Creeds of Christendom* (Grand Rapids: Baker, 1910), Decree on Justification, Chapter VII, Canons X, XXXII.

[49]*The Canons and Decrees of the Council of Trent*. Found in Philip Schaff, *The Creeds of Christendom* (Grand Rapids: Baker, 1910), Decree on Justification, Chapter VII, Canons X, XXXII.

[50]Ludwig Ott, *Fundamentals of Catholic Dogma* (Rockford: Tan, 1974), pp.254, 264.

[51]John Hardon, *The Question and Answer Catholic Catechism* (Garden City: Image, 1981), Question #1074.

[52]*The Canons and Decrees of the Council of Trent*. Found in Philip Schaff, *The Creeds of Christendom* (Grand Rapids: Baker, 1910), Decree on Justification, Chapter XVI, Canon IX.

[53]*Justification by Faith Alone*, Don Kistler, Ed. (Morgan: Soli Deo Gloria, 1995), John Gerstner, *The Nature of Justifying Faith*, pp. 111–113.

[54]*Dogmatic Decrees of the Vatican Council*, On Faith, Chapter III. Found in Philip Schaff, *The Creeds of Christendom* (New York:Harper, 1877), Volume II, pp. 244-245.

[55]Ludwig Ott, *Fundamentals of Catholic Dogma* (Rockford: Tan, 1974), pp. 4-5, 253.

[56]John Hardon, *The Question and Answer Catholic Catechism* (Garden City: Image, 1981), Questions #44, 45, 46, 47.

[57]*Dogmatic Decrees of the Vatican Council*. Found in *The Creeds of Christendom* by Philip Schaff (Grand Rapids: Baker, 1910), Chapter III, On the Power and Nature of the Primacy of the Roman Pontiff.

[58]John Calvin, *Institutes of the Christian Religion*. Found in *The Library of Christian Classics* (Philadelphia: Westminster, 1960), Volume XIX, Book III, Ch. XVI.1, p. 798.

[59]Martin Luther, *Concerning Christian Liberty*. Found in *Luther's Primary Works* (London: Hodder & Stroughton, 1896), Henry Wace and C.A. Buchheim Ed.,, pp. 275-277, 288.

[60]*The Confession of Faith*, Cap. XIII, *The Cause of Good Works*. Found in *John Knox's History of the Reformation in Scotland* (New York: Philisophical Library, 1950), Volume II, p. 263.

[61]*The Westminster Confession of Faith*. Found in A.A. Hodge, *The Confession of Faith* (Edinburgh: Banner, 1958), p. 204.

[62]A.A. Hodge, *Evangelical Theology* (Edinburgh: Banner, 1976), p. 297.

[63]Martyn Lloyd-Jones, *Sanctified Through the Truth* (Westchester: Crossway, 1989), p. 86, 85, 91, 77.

[64]J.I. Packer, *God's Words* (Downers Grove: InterVarsity), p. 74.

[65]*The New International Dictionary of New Testament Theology* (Grand Rapids: Zondervan, 1978), Volume III, pp. 592-593, 597, 596.

[66]John Murray, *Collected Writings of John Murray* (Edinburgh: Banner, 1977), Volume 2, pp. 278-280.

[67]John Owen, *The Works of John Owen* (Edinburgh: Banner, 1965), Volume 1, p. 136; Volume 3, pp. 480–481.

[68]John Flavel, *The Works of John Flavel* (Edinburgh: Banner, 1968), Volume II, Sermon I, *The Method of Grace*, p. 19.

[69]William Marshner, *Justification by Faith*. Taken from *Reasons for Hope: Catholic Apologetics* (Front Royal: Christendom College, 1978), p. 237.

[70]*Justification by Faith Alone*, Don Kistler, Ed. (Morgan: Soli Deo Gloria, 1995), John Gerstner, *The Nature of Justifying Faith*, pp. 113–115.

[71]D.M. Lloyd–Jones, *Darkness and Light: An Exposition of Ephesians 4:17-5:17* (Grand Rapids: Baker, 1982), pp. 350-351, 353.

[72]D.A. Carson, *The Gospel According To John* (Grand Rapids: Eerdmans, 19910, pp. 189-190.

[73]John Murray, *Collected Writings of John Murray* (Edinburgh: Banner, 1977), Volume 2, pp. 171-172.

[74]John Calvin, *Institutes of the Christian Religion*. Found in *The Library of Christian Classics* (Philadelphia: Westminster, 1960), Volume XIX, Book III, Chp. XI.6,11; pp. 732, 739.

[75]Huldrych Zwingli, *Commentary On True and False Religion* (Durham: Labyrinth, 1981), p. 120.

[76]Philip Melanchthon, *Loci Communes Theologici*. Found in *The Library of Christian Classics* (Philadelphia: Westminster, 1969), Volume XIX, p. 123.

[77]*Justification by Faith Alone*, Don Kistler, Ed. (Morgan: Soli Deo Gloria, 1995), *The Forensic Nature of Justification*, pp. 43-45.

[78]D.A. Carson, *The Gospel According To John* (Grand Rapids: Eerdmans, 1991), p. 198.

[79]D. Martyn Lloyd–Jones, *Romans: Atonement and Justification* (Grand Rapids: Zondervan,1970), pp. 184-85.

[80]John Calvin, *Institutes of the Christian Religion*. Found in *The Library of Christian Classics* (Philadelphia: Westminster, 1960), Volume XXI, pp. 1304–1305.

[81]Charles Hodge, *Systematic Theology,* Volume III, p. 52I.

[82]Charles Hodge, *Systematic Theology,* Volume III, p. 601.

[83]Matthew Henry, *Matthew Henry's Commentary on the Whole Bible* (Old Tappan: Revell), Volume 6, pp. I026–27.

[84]Huldrych Zwingli, *Of Baptism.* Found in *The Library of Christian Classics* (Philadelphia: Westminster, 1953), Volume XXIV, pp. 136–137, 156.

[85]John Hooper, *A Declaration of Christe and His Offyce.* Found in *The Library of Christian Classics* (Philadelphia: Westminster, 1966), Volume XXVI, pp. 210–211.

[86]John Murray, *Collected Writings of John Murray* (Edinburgh: Banner, 1977), Volume 2, pp. 182–84.

[87]D.A. Carson, *The Gospel According To john* (Grand Rapids: Eerdmans, 1991), p. 202.

[88]John Calvin, *Institutes of the Christian Religion.* Found in *The Library of Christian Classics* (Philadelphia: Westminster, 1960), pp. 1304–1305.

[89]Louis Berkhof, *Systematic Theology* (Grand Rapids: Eerdmans, 1939), p. 450.

[90]R.L. Dabney, *Systematic Theology*(Grand Rapids: Zondervan, 1980), p. 615.

[91]John Murray, *Collected Writings of John Murray* (Edinburgh: Banner, 1977), Volume 2, p. 197.

[92]John Calvin, *Institutes of the Christian Religion.* Found in *The Library of Christian Classics* (Philadelphia: Westminster, 1960), Volume XIX, Book III, Chapters 1, 5, pp. 592-593, 597.

[93]Huldrych Zwingli, *Commentary On True and False Religion* (Durham: Labyrinth, 1981), pp. 131–132.

[94]Martin Bucer, *On the Kingdom of Christ.* Found in *The Library of Christian Classics* (Philadelphia: Westminster, 1969), Volume XIX, p. 219.

[95]Thomas Watson, *The Doctrine of Repentance* (Edinburgh: Banner, 1987), pp. 12–13, 59, 77.

[96]Louis Berkhof, *Systematic Theology* (Grand Rapids: Eerdmans, 1939), p. 492.

[97]John Murray, *Redemption Accomplished and Applied* (Grand Rapids: Eerdmans, 1955), p. 113.

[98]*The Westminster Confession of Faith*, Chapter XV, Sections I and II. Cited in A.A. Hodge, *The Confession of Faith* (Edinburgh: Banner, 1958), p. 210.

[99]R.L. Dabney, *Systematic Theology* (Grand Rapids: Zondervan, 1980), pp.

606-607.

[100]R.L. Dabney, *Systematic Theology* (Grand Rapids: Zondervan, 1980), p. 651.

[101]John Calvin, *Institutes of the Christian Religion*. Found in *The Library of Christian Classics* (Philadelphia: Westminster, 1960), Volume XIX, Book III.3. 5-6, 16, pp. 597-598, 609-610.

[102]John Richard deWitt, *Amazing Love* (Edinburgh: Banner, 1981), pp. 66,74-76.

[103]A.A. Hodge, *The Confession of Faith* (Edinburgh: Banner, 1958), pp. 212–213.

[104]Charles Hodge, *The Way of Life* (Edinburgh: Banner, 1959), pp. 153, 166-169.

[105]A.W. Pink, *The Doctrine of Salvation* (Grand Rapids: Baker, 1975), pp.45, 49-53, 56, 58, 60, 79.Jonathan Edwards

[106]Jonathan Edwards, *The Works of Jonathan Edwards* Edinburgh: Banner, 1974), Volume 2, Discourse: *Men Naturally are God's Enemies,* pp. 132, 138-139.

[107]John Owen, *The Works of John Owen* (Edinburgh: Banner, 1967), Volume 8, pp. 635–636.

[108]C.H. Spurgeon, *Metropolitan Tabernacle Pulpit* (Edinburgh: Banner, 1970), Volume 35, p. 127.

[109]B.B. Warfield, *Selected Shorter Writings - 1* (Nutley: Presbyterian & Reformed, 1970), pp. 279-280.

[110]*Justification By Faith Alone*, Don Kistler, Ed., (Morgan: Soli Deo Gloria, 1995), pp. 55–56, 58–61.

[111]Martin Luther, *On Translating: An Open Letter*. Found in *A Compend of Luther's Theology* (Philadelphia: Westminster, 1966), pp. 100–102.

[112]Don Kistler, Ed., *Justification by Faith Alone* (Morgan: Soli Deo Gloria, 1995), pp. 106, 110.

[113]John Calvin, *Institutes of the Christian Religion*. Found in *The Library of Christian Classics* (Philadelphia: Westminster, 1960), Book III, Ch. XI.7, p. 733.

[114]John Calvin, *Institutes of the Christian Religion*. Found in *The Library of Christian Classics* (Philadelphia: Westminster, 1960), Book III, Ch. XI.1, p. 725.

[115]John Calvin, *Institutes of the Christian Religion*. Found in *The Library of Christian Classics* (Philadelphia: Westminster, 1960), Book III, Ch. II.8, p.

552.

[116]John Flavel, *The Works of John Flavel* (Edinburgh: Banner, 1968), Volume II, Sermon I, *The Method of Grace,* p. 17.

[117]A.A. Hodge, *Evangelical Theology* (Edinburgh: Banner, 1976), p. 120.

[118]Louis Berkhof, *Systematic Theology* (Grand Rapids: Eerdmans, 1939), p. 495-496.

[119]Louis Berkhof, *Systematic Theology* (Grand Rapids: Eerdmans, 1939), p. 520.

[120]Louis Berkhof, *Systematic Theology* (Grand Rapids: Eerdmans, 1939), p. 522.

[121]Louis Berkhof, *Systematic Theology* (Grand Rapids: Eerdmans, 1939), p. 505.

[122]*The Westminster Confession of Faith,* Chapter XIV, Section II. Found in A.A. Hodge, *The Confession of Faith,* (Edinburgh: Banner, 1958), p. 204.

[123]John Flavel, *The Works of John Flavel* (Edinburgh: Banner, 1968), Volume 2, pp. 102-105, 107-112, 115, 122-123, 140.

[124]Louis Berkhof, *Systematic Theology* (Grand Rapids: Eerdmans, 1939), pp. 503-505.

[125]John Calvin, *Institutes of the Christian Religion.* Found in *The Library of Christian Classics* (Philadelphia: Westminster, 1960), Book III, Ch. II.8, pp. 552-553.

[126]A.A. Hodge, *Evangelical Theology* (Edinburgh: Banner, 1976), pp. 120, 233.

[127]R.C. Sproul, *Faith Alone* (Grand Rapids: Baker, 1995), pp. 88-90.

[128]R.C. Sproul, *Faith Alone* (Grand Rapids: Baker, 1995), p. 90.

[129] John Murray, *Collected Writings of John Murray* (Edinburgh: Banner, 1974), Volume 2., pp. 220-221.

[130]John Murray, *Collected Writings of John Murray* (Edinburgh: Banner, 1974), Volume 2, pp. 257-260.

[131]R.L. Dabney, *Systematic Theology* (Edinburgh: Banner, 1871) p. 601.

[132]Thomas Watson, *The Godly Man's Picture* (Edinburgh: Banner, 1992), p. 22.

[133]John Calvin, *Institutes of the Christian Religion.* Found in *The Library of Christian Classics* (Philadelphia: Westminster, 1960), Book III, Ch. XI.10, pp. 736-737.

[134]D.M. Lloyd Jones, *The Puritans: Their Origins and Successors* (Edinburgh: Banner, 1987), pp. 27, 31-32, 36, 51, 49.

[135]John Murray, *Collected Writings of John Murray* (Edinburgh: Banner, 1977), Volume 2, pp. 170, 202.

[136]Louis Berkhof, *Systematic Theology* (Grand Rapids: Eerdmans, 1939), pp. 480-481, 483, 485, 491-492.

[137]Jonathan Edwards, *A Treatise Concerning Religious Affections*. Found in *The Works of Jonathan Edwards* (Edinburgh: Banner, 1974), Volume I, pp. 294–295.

[138]John Murray, *Collected Writings of John Murray* (Edinburgh: Banner, 1977), Volume 2, pp. 262-263.

[139]B.B. Warfield, *Faith & Life* (Edinburgh: Banner, 1974), p. 176.

[140]J.I. Packer, *Evangelism and the Sovereignty of God* (Downers Grove: InterVarsity, 1961), pp. 71-73, 88-89.

[141]Harold O.J. Brown, *Unhelpful Antagonism and Unhealthy Courtesy*. Found in *Roman Catholicism: Evangelical Protestants Analyze What Divides and What Unites Us* (Chicago: Moody, 1994), John Armstrong, Ed., p. 169.

[142]William Hendriksen, *New Testament Commentary, The Gospel of Luke* (Grand Rapids: Baker, 1978), pp. 734-735.

[143]G. Campbell Morgan, *The Westminster Pulpit*, (Grand Rapids: Baker, 1954) Volume I, pp. 43-44.

[144]William Hendriksen, *New Testament Commentary, The Gospel of Luke*, p. 737.

[145]John Stott, *Basic Christianity* (Grand Rapids: Eerdmans, 1972), p. 111.

[146]John Stott, *Basic Christianity* (Grand Rapids: Eerdmans, 1972), pp. 111-112.

[147]R.C.H. Lenski, *Interpretation of St. Mark's Gospel* (Minneapolis: Augsburg, 1961), p. 348.

[148]William Hendriksen, *New Testament Commentary, The Gospel of Mark* (Grand Rapids: Baker, 1975), p. 330.

[149]William Hendriksen, *New Testament Commentary, The Gospel of Luke* (Grand Rapids: Baker, 1978), pp. 498-500.

[150]James Montgomery Boice, *Christ's Call to Discipleship* (Chicago: Moody, 1986), p. 19.

[151]F.F. Bruce, *The Gospel of John* (Grand Rapids: Eerdmans, 1983), p. 265.

[152]D.A. Carson, *The Gospel According to John* (Grand Rapids: Eerdmans, 1991), pp. 438-439.

[153]Walter Chantry, *Today's Gospel—Synthetic or Authentic?* (Edinburgh: Banner, 1970), pp. 55, 59-60.

[154]D. M. Lloyd–Jones, *Sermon on the Mount* (Grand Rapids: Eerdmans, 1981), Vol. 2, pp. 221, 224-225, 248-249.

[155]Jonathan Edwards, *The Works of Jonathan Edwards*, Volume 2, Discourse: *Men Naturally are God's Enemies*, pp. 132, 138-139.

[156]J.I. Packer, *Evagelism and the Sovereignty of God* (Downers Grove: InterVarsity, 1961), p. 72.

[157]James Montgomery Boice, *Christ's Call to Discipleship* (Chicago: Moody, 1986), pp. 13, 14, 16, 21.

[158]A. W. Tozer, *I Call It Heresy* (Camp Hill:Christian Publications, 1974), pp. 9, 14-16. 18-20.

[159]James Montgomery Boice, *Christ's Call to Discipleship* (Chicago: Moody, 1986), p. 21.

[160]J.I. Packer, Comments from the Foreword to *The Gospel According to Jesus* by John MacArthur (Grand Rapids: Zondervan, 1988), p. ix.

[161]*The Westminster Confession of Faith,* Chapter XIV, Section II. Found in A.A. Hodge, *The Confession of Faith*, (Edinburgh: Banner, 1958), p. 204.

[162]John Owen, *The Works of John Owen* (Edinburgh: Banner, 1965), Volume 1, p. 136; Volume 3, pp. 480–481.

[163]John Murray, *Redemption Accomplished and Applied* (Grand Rapids: Eerdmans, 1955), p. 113.

[164]Thomas Watson, *The Doctrine of Repentance* (Edinburgh: Banner, 1987), p. 77.

[165]R.L. Dabney, *Systematic Theology* (Edinburgh: Banner, 1871) p. 664.

[166]James Montgomery Boice, *Christ's Call to Discipleship* (Chicago: Moody, 1986), pp. 15-16.

[167]Thomas Cranmer, *A Short Declaration of the True, Lively and Christian Faith*. Found in *The Library of Christian Classics* (Philadelphia: Westminster, 1966), Volume XXVI, pp. 277, 280–281.

[168]John Hooper, *A Declaration of Christe and His Offyce*. Found in *The Library of Christian Classics* (Philadelphia: Westminster, 1966), Volume XXVI, p. 198.